Joseph Wise

A Miscellany of Poems

Joseph Wise

A Miscellany of Poems

ISBN/EAN: 9783744772303

Printed in Europe, USA, Canada, Australia, Japan

Cover: Foto ©Thomas Meinert / pixelio.de

More available books at **www.hansebooks.com**

A

MISCELLANY

OF

POEMS,

By the Reverend

JOSEPH WISE,

Rector of Penhurst, Sussex.

LONDON:

Printed for the Author, and sold by Messrs. Dilly in the Poultry, Robson in New Bond Street, Cadell in the Strand, Flexney in Holborn, and Evans in Pater-noster-Row.

MDCCLXXV.

LIST
OF
SUBSCRIBERS.

A

Robert Armitage, Esq; East-Barnet, Herts
Rev. Mr. Atkinson, 6 copies
Mr. William Atkinson, Southwark

B

Mrs. Braithwaite
Mr. John Barwise, A. M. Soho Square
Mr. Thomas Boak, Haymarket
Mrs. Bacon, Bloomsbury
Mrs. Brownsworth
Rev. Mr. Bishop
Mr. Bowzer, Fair-Street, Southwark
John Ballard, Esq; Dacre-Street, Westm.
Mrs. Ballard
Rev. Mr. Thomas Bull, Manuden, Essex
Mr. Rich. Barnes, Supervisor, Waltham-Abby, Es.

Mr. Briscoe, Little-Tower-Street, 2 copies
Rev. Mr. John Bulman
Mr. John Braithwaite, Maryport, Cumberland
Mr. Thomas Barwise, Dubmill, Cumberland
Rev. Mr. Baxter, Brother of the Collegiate Church
    of St. Katherine, 7 copies

C

Right Rev. Lord Bishop of Carlisle
Rev. Mr. Clarke, Holborn, 50 copies
Mr. Clarke, 2 copies
Miss Colleton
Mrs. Colleton
James Nassau Colleton, Esq;
George William Carrington, Esq;
Mr. Churchill, Parliament-Street, 50 copies
Mr. Corneck
Mr. Campbell
Mr. Chapman, Strand
Mrs. Chapman, Redlion-Street
Mrs. Court
    Clare, Esq;
Mr. Newell Connop, Enfield-Highway, Middx.
Mr. Corney, Surgeon, Southwark
Rev. Mr. Chambers, Allhallows, Cumberland
James Craik, Esq; Flembye, Cumberland

D

Mrs. Dancer, Barnet, Herts
Miss E. D.
Miss Frances Davenport
Dr. Ducarel, Commissary of the Collegiate Church of St. Katherine, 2 copies

E

Mr. Joseph Earle

F

John Forbes, Esq;
John Forbes, Esq; Temple
Keane Fitzgerald, Esq; Inner-Temple
John Fasset, Esq; Fair-Street, Southwark, 3 copies
Mrs. Fasset, 3 copies
Rev. Dr. Finch, Guy's Hospital, 3 copies
Mr. Joseph Fell, Mary-port, Cumberland
Mr. Daniel Fisher, Mary-port, Cumberland
Mrs. Fulham, St. Katherine

G

Miss Gore
Rev. Mr. Brown Grisdale, Carlisle
Mr. Simon Grayson, Mary-port, Cumberland

[iv]

Rev. Mr. Joseph Gilbanks, junior, Mary-port, Cumberland
Mr. William Gilby, Southwark

H

Jonas Hanway, Esq; 2 copies
Miss Hector Harris
William Henry Higden, Esq;
Mr. Harris, Surgeon
Capt. Haly
Rev. Mr. Hazard, B. A. Lincoln College, Oxford, Chaplain to the Right Honourable Lord Lyttleton
John Hanway, Esq; Cheapside
Mr. Richard Holiday, Mary-port, Cumberland
Mr. Samuel Hollingsworth, Southwark
Mr. William Haddon, Southwark
Mr. Thomas Hearne, Southwark
Rev. Mr. Hinton, Brother of the Collegiate Church of St. Katherine, 3 copies
Mrs. Hayley, 7 copies

J

Miss Jenkenson, Hoxton
Miss Matilda Jenkenson, Hoxton
Mr. Joseph Johnson, St. Paul's-Church-yard
Rev. Mr. Nathanael Jennings, Islington

K

Mrs. Keene, Hertford-Street, May-Fair
Miss Keene, ditto
Mrs. Knight, St. Katherine

L

Mr. Lewellin
Edmund Lechmore, Esq; Barister at law, Inner Temple
Mr. Lobb, 2 copies
Mr. Lyon, Surgeon, Clerkenwell
Mr. William Lister, Southwark
Rev. Mr. John Law

M

Mr. Marriot, Cheapside
Rev. Dr. Markham, 3 copies
Mrs. Mallet
Dr. Merrish, Chelmsford
Mr. William Mason, Waltham-Abby, Essex
Mr. Thomas Mitchell, Mary-port Cumberland
Mr. Thomas Millar, Cowper, Cumberland

N

Charles Neate, Esq; Whetstone
Miss Neate, Whetstone

Mr. Thomas Needs, Queen-Street, Lincoln's-Inn-Fields
Mr. John Nelson, Mary-port, Cumberland
Mr. Philip Nelson, junior, Mary-port, Cumberland
Mr. Andrew Newland, Southwark

P

Right Rev. Lord Bishop of Peterborough
Rev. Mr. Pigot, Vicar of Ridge, Herts
Miss Plukenett, East-Barnet
Mr. Peate, 2 copies
Mr. Thomas Plaskett
Mr. Payne, St. James's
Mr. John Payne, Gray's-Inn
Rev. Samuel Pickering, A. M. New-Street, Spring-Gardens
Rev. Mr. Popham, Strand
Mr. Pardon, Blackman-Street, Southwark
Mr. Thomas Postlethwaite, Mary-port, Cumberland
Mrs. Pearce, St. Katherine
Commelin Pigou, Esq;

R

George Randall, Esq;
William Richardson, Esq; Mount-pleasant, Herts

Mr. Ritson, Collector of Excise
Mr. Righton, St. Katherine

S

Jeremy Sneyd, Esq;
Joseph Senhouse, Esq; Arundel-Street, Strand
Mrs. Sumner, Dock-Head
Mrs. Singleton
Mrs. Smith, Cursitor-Street
Mrs. Shaw
Rev. Dr. Sclater, Greville-Street
Mr. John Scott
Rev. Mr. Stapylton, Brother of the Collegiate Church of St. Katherine
Rev. P. Sandiford
Mr. John Sturges, Southwark

T

Miss Thomlinson, Hertford-Street, May-Fair
Miss M. Thomlinson, Hertford-Street, May-Fair
Mr. Thornthwaite, St. Paul's Church-yard, 4 cop.
Rev. Mr. Temple
Mr. Thomas Thornthwaite, 2 copies
Mr. Jonathan Thornthwaite, Allonby, Cumberland
Rev. Mr. Thomas

U

Rev. Mr. Underwood, Rector of Barnet, Herts

W

Mrs. Wagstaff, Great Barford, Bedfordshire

Rev. Mr. Ward, Fellow Queen's College, Cambridgeshire

Mr. Watson, Mincing-Lane, 36 copies

Rev. Mr. Winstanley, Prebendary of St. Paul's, 4 copies

Mrs. Winstanley, 7 copies

Rev. Mr. Waite, Bromfield, Cumberland

Mr. William Wood, Mary-port, Cumberland

Mr. Benjamin Wise, Apothecary, Mary-port, Cumberland

Mr. John Wilson, Mary-port, Cumberland

Mr. John Wise, Hartlaw, Cumberland

Edmund Waller, Esq;

Mr. Robert Wise.

ERRATA.

Page	line	
10	15	for *repeating* r. *repenting.*
27	17	*yet,* r. *get.*
33	8	*Enipcus,* r. *Enipeus.*
44	16	*emyloy,* r. *employ.*
49	24	*feated,* r. *fealed.*
55	5	r. *with* a senseless joy.

A MISCELLANY OF POEMS.

The INTRODUCTION.

SEE the GODDESS MUSE descend!
   All ye minstrelsy of song,
   At her gentle side attend;
Hallow'd virgins come along!

   Sober *Silence*, solemn guest!
Solitude, thou pensive maid!
Calm *Content*, forever blest!
Tend her thro' the sylvan shade.

   Fancy gay, her train adorn
In the airy walks of flow'rs!
Smile, soft pearly-eyed *Morn!*
Music, warble in her bowr's!

Piety,

Piety, with flaming wing;
Hope, with aspect ever fair,
Your celestial nectar bring,
Surest anodyne of care.

Happy *raptures*, ever warm;
Generous *ardors*, ever glow;
Life without you knows no charm;
Nature is a waste of woe.

Pleasure drop the harlot smile;
Modest in her train appear:
Folly hence; and odious *Guile*,
Tremble at Ithuriel's spear *.

Welcome in thy native white,
Young-ey'd *Innocence*; with thee,
Blythe in robes of silver light,
Mildly sweet *Simplicity*.

Circled thus, ye FAIR! behold
Majesty poetic tread,
Blazing in a cloud of gold,
Starry-crown'd her beauteous head.

Twine your chaplets, strew your roses;
Rev'rence your auspicious guest!
While

---

* See MILTON's Paradise Lost, Book IV. line 810.

While she studiously composes,
Pleasures for each gentle breast.

ODE XIII.

BOOK I. Of HORACE.

Resembling the celebrated Ode of SAPPHO.

O *Liddy*, while you praise the charms,
   The rosy neck, the waxen arms
Of gentle *Teleph*—woe my heart!
It swells and burns with bitter smart.
My reason lost, my color gone,
A starting tear distilling down,
Are symptoms sad of fierce desire;
The raging glow of jealous fire.
Your lily bosom, softly fine,
Has he besotly stain'd with wine,
Your ruby lip has he impress'd,
What madding anguish stings my breast!

  But O my kind suggestion hear!
He will not, cannot, be sincere;
You'll quickly lose a fop, like this,
Who rudely spoils the balmy kiss,
Which Venus, wantonly profuse,
Dip'd thrice in rich nectareous dews.

Superlatively

Superlatively bleſt, and more,
Are they whoſe raptures know no ſhore;
Whoſe paſſion ſanctify'd from ſtrife,
Will only terminate with life.

The CELEBRATED ODE *of* SAPPHO.

SOME youthful God in blooming pride
   Seems he to me, as by your ſide
He ſits, and ay to you, by whiles,
So fondly whiſpers, ſweetly ſmiles.

That moment, *Sappho*, ſick'ning, felt
Her heart within her boſom melt.

Ah, when I look'd on thee, too bleſt,
A riſing ſob my voice ſuppreſs'd;
My tongue relax'd; a ſudden glow
Thro' all my nerves did, trembling, flow:
My eyes grew dim, my ears did knell,
My blood did thrill; I turn'd more pale
Than blighted ozier; faint I lay;
My very life diſſolv'd away.

Yet ſhall not hope forſake my breaſt,
Tho' poorly ſlighted and depreſs'd.

SAPPHO's

Sappho's HYMN to Venus.

O Mighty *Venus!* Queen divine!
  Intriguing princess of the skies!
Regard a Votary of thine,
Oppress'd with sorrow, faint with sighs.

  Hear, I adjure by Love's dread pow'r!
My wonted voice, you oft did hear,
When, leaving Jove's imperial tow'r,
You deign'd to banish all my fear.

  Your pretty sparrows quiv'ring flew
Along the still pellucid air,
As you in lovely pomp they drew,
All-smiling in your pearly chair.

  Soon did you light; your birds return;
Divinely courteous, then you said,
" Why does my darling *Sappho* mourn?
" Why calls my charmer for my aid?

  " Say whence this tender phrenzy rose?
" Ah, whom shall soft perswasion move?
" Or whom Love's silken net inclose?
" What cruel youth slights *Sappho*'s love?
            " Tho'

"Tho' now he shuns, he shall pursue;
"Tho' presents scorns, shall presents give;
"Tho' he disdains, he soon shall bow,
"And humbly your commands receive."

Once more, O goddess! quell my grief;
Appease the torments of despair:
Vouchsafe my soul divine relief,
Thou potent queen of am'rous war!

ODE XLVI.

Of ANACREON.

WITHOUT love 'tis pain to live;
    Love itself much pain doth give:
O, but greatest is the pain,
Still to love and never gain.

Beauty slights the noble born;
Spurns the wise and good with scorn;
Gold, the dear unrival'd prize,
Charms alone all charming eyes.

Perish wretch! whose bosom vile,
First admir'd the shining soil.

Brothers

Brothers thence no brother know;
Parents thence no parents grow:
Murders, wars, diſtruſt, diſguiſe,
Hateful paſſions thence ariſe:
Worſt of all, vile gold deſtroys
Noble love, with all its joys.

ODE III.

BOOK I. Of Horace,

(Intreating a proſperous Voyage for his Friend Virgil) imitated.

NOW, to guide the floating keel,
    Brighteſt Conſtellations, glow!
Boiſterous Boreas, peace, be ſtill!
All propitious Breezes blow!

    Swiftly waft the veſſel o'er,
O'er the rough and rapid wave;
Safely waft her keel aſhore:
Half my ſoul defend and ſave!

    Adamant and braſs did fold
Thrice his daring boſom round,
Who, in ſlender veſſel, bold,
Ventur'd firſt the wild profound.

Dreaded

Dreaded He the furious blast,
When the south and north engage,
When black tempests overcast,
And tremendous thunders rage?

Fear'd he death in all its forms,
Who, unmov'd, sea-monsters saw,
Tumbling billows, howling storms,
And the pointed rocks below?

God in vain with seas divides
Rival realms, unfriendly shores,
While on the forbidden tides
Speed our impious sails and oars.

Bold and enterprizing man
Rushes on to ev'ry ill:
Father *Adam*, in the van,
Stole the fruit, ordain'd to kill.

Since he dar'd that deed of shame,
Violating love and fear,
Swarms of strange diseases came,
Seiz'd on earth, and settled here.

Far behind, at first, and slow
Death pursu'd the human race;
Now

Now no more he loiters so;
Vengeance bids him mend his pace.

Grandeur, graciously deny'd,
Babel-architects explor'd;
Some, with more amazing pride,
Sought to be as Gods ador'd.

Nothing's human views above;
Folly tempts the very sky.
Sin will never suffer Jove
To lay his glowing thunders by.

ODE IV.

BOOK I. Of HORACE, imitated.

NOW vernal sun-shine, milder breezes
  Dissipate the winter's cold:
A cloister'd life no longer pleases,
Since the rural scenes unfold.

Gay Love leads forth, with song and dancing,
All the tenants of the plain;
And Beauty, virgin-like advancing,
Chears and charms the soul of man.

Love, praise and thankful adoration
To the glorious God are due,
Who made, sustains, adorns creation,
Painting Nature's scenes anew.

Grim Death with equal pace approaches
Cots of clowns and courts of kings:
The brevity of life reproaches
Hopes prolong'd in transient things.

What mortal knows, O friend beloved!
Who Death's victim next shall fall?
Most happy he, if well approved
By the Lord and Judge of all.

Be wise, the worst of ills preventing;
Now the path of life explore!
When trial's past is no repenting;
Grace withdraws, and hope's no more.

The MORNING.

NOW smiles the morning; fresh the verdure seems,
Bepearl'd with dew: The shining silver streams
Glide most delightful: all the feather'd choir
To swell the voice of general joy conspire:
The Sun, grand fountain of ethereal rays,
From the horizon pours a golden blaze.

Far the wide ocean of his fulgence shews
The pow'r and goodness of the Sovereign Cause;
And at the view, lo, general Nature, gay,
Rises to hail the Lord of new-born day.

While the creation labors thus to raise
(And all too weak!) the high Creator's praise.
Shall man be silent, lordly man, so blest
With dignity and favor o'er the rest?
Will favor'd man no gratitude repay
For love, which lights the glorious orb of day?
For love, which pours the treasures of the soil,
The sweets of ease, and the rewards of toil?
For love, which bow'd th' eternal heav'ns, and join'd
The Lord of glory with the humankind?
Consider this, ye sons of dust! and raise
Your loftiest anthems to your Maker's praise.

Behold how Nature gradually descends!
On just connexion, like a chain, suspends:
The moral kinds in blissful order move,
Rul'd and connected by the pow'r of love:
Combin'd by love, that universal law,
Bond of perfection, fountain pure, whence flow
The social harmonies, the virtues bright,
Religion holy—all the train of light.
Will man this sacred principle destroy,
In him the taste, in God the spring of joy?

Will

Will man, forsaking Nature's reason's rule,
Expose the reas'ner a delib'rate fool?
Consider this, ye sons of dust! and raise
Your holiest raptures to your Maker's praise.

At first, the wise, just, good, eternal Mind
His noble works from evil free design'd:
Order and peace once reign'd throughout the whole
Soundness of body, happiness of soul:
(Thus reason's voice—It must be understood;
Else how is God or wise, or just, or good?)
Immortal life had joys immortal known,
Bliss and perfection, love and duty one;
Had man not sinn'd, by Satan's guile betray'd,
And suffer'd justly for the choice, he made.
To prove how heinous sin, the curse descends;
And but thro' trial and redemption ends.
Consider this, ye sons of dust! and know
How good, how sacred, is the perfect law.

Now feeble enmity, sustain'd by pride,
And glimmering reason, man's bewilder'd guide,
Self-guarding and self-guiding, but expose
The wretched being to endless crimes and woes;
Until the holy *Spirit*, wing'd with light,
Oe'r-shadow man with sanctifying might;
His health restore, from second chaos born;
And all his soul with righteousness adorn.

To gain this boon was *Christ* content to die,
At once to reconcile and sanctify.
Consider this, ye sons of dust! and pray
For that best gift, a sanctifying ray.

Nor think, that Grace resistless aid imparts,
To guide men's judgments, or to mend their hearts:
But like the Sun, which vital radiance sheds
O'er humble vales and lofty mountain-heads,
It shines on all sufficient,—oft in vain!
Unless you till the soil, expect no grain:
The talents giv'n with diligence improve;
Or hope no new accessions from above.
Or strong, or weak, or bright, or dull thy mind,
To serve the Maker was the work design'd:
To his high glory bend thy strength and skill;
So grace shall wing thy thought, and nerve thy will.
Consider this, ye sons of dust, and rise
With ev'ry faculty to meet the skies.

An IRREGULAR ODE.

DUST *to dust!*—O solemn found!
This florid, active, curious frame
Shortly must lose life, form and name;
And be no more than common ground.

With titles honor'd, and in badges dress'd,
In council wise, in fields of slaughter brave,
The Great, our mortal Gods, like all the rest,
Must sink dishonor'd in the gloomy grave.

The medal and the sumptuous bust
At length will crumble into dust:
All the arts of fame decay;
All the hopes of pride betray;
And all to void oblivion die away!

" Luxury, open all thy stores,
" Genial charms, indulgent pow'rs;
" With careless Plenty, wanton Ease,
" Splendor's ev'ry grace to please,
" With Beauty, Music, Dance and Song,
" Charming Luxury! come along!
" Life is short; and all its treasure
" Is a little fleeting pleasure:
" Fame's a breath and Virtue vain:
" Let Indolence, let Pleasure reign!

What!—paltry Joy! inglorious Ease!
Sense indulge, and Reason quit!
Is it spirit, is it wit
To sink in folly and disease?

Do such delights beseem the wise?
Ah, where is truth? where social ties?
Is there no high reversion in the skies?
" 'Tis

" 'Tis wife to follow nature's road;
" For nature is the law of God."
Ah, what but God's and reason's voice
Shall mark the path, decide the choice?
 Sense deprav'd, and reason blind,
 Wretched is the human mind:
 But this by all confess'd is still,
 Whate'er does mischief must be ill:
 Consequences ever prove
 The bad of selfish, good of social love.

 Superlatively blest are they,
Who, nobly passion'd, scorn to stay!
As saints mature, so mortals here
Find bliss alone in Virtue's sphere.
 Woe to Av'rice, Pride and Lust,
When white-rob'd Priest pronounces--"*Dust to dust.*"

HEAVEN.

FROM real scenes, obscure and dull,
 Softly stole, my Fancy play
'mong fair ideals, where in full
Bloom the lovliest tints of May.

 We clasp each dear deceit, that brings
Fancy'd joy, dispelling care;
Then, Fancy, wave thy rosy wings;
Lightly revel, light as air.
      O Waft

O Waft me from this guilty vale;
Waft me to that happy shore,
Where humble Innocence shall dwell;
Holy Charities adore;

Zeal, Gratitude and Rev'rence meek,
See the uncreated Light;
And hear the awful G L O R Y speak,
Ravish'd with bliss infinite.

The time approaches, when this world
Shall, like us its dwellers, fall;
And, all to second chaos hurl'd,
Conflagration swallow all.

Then, at the voice of God shall rise,
From the ruins of the old,
A new bright earth and happy skies,
An eternal age of gold,

This heavenly fabric shall display
Scenes transcendently sublime,
Which not thro' boundless years decay,
Beauties never chang'd with time.

Here rocks of diamond, meads of roses,
Groves of cedar, myrtle shades,
Where Health still wanders and reposes,
Pleasure sports with all her maids,

Of herbs and flow'rs, to fight and smell
Rich and rare, the carpet lies;
Ambrosian fragrance these exhale,
These delight admiring eyes.

Large rivers, clear as chryſtal, flow,
Murmuring on the pearly bed:
Balmy breezes whiſpering blow,
Juſt to wave the Pine-tree's head.

Here walls of Jaſper, tow'rs of Beryl,
Heav'nly architecture, ſhine:
High domes of chryſolite and pearl
Glitter on the plains divine.

Theſe are the bleſt hierarchal ſeats,
Where magnificence abounds;
Where innocence with pleaſure meets,
Holy muſic ever ſounds.

Here Muſes with inſpired ſkill
Sing; while Muſic tunes her voice;
With melody all ether fill:
All the bleſſed Choirs rejoice.

No ſun nor moon with changing light
Scatters groſs intemp'rate rays;
But God's own Glory ſhuts out Night,
Beaming with unclouded blaze.

Here shall the Saints, from Death restor'd,
Chang'd to Seraph-forms, be blest
More than e'er Eye or Ear explor'd,
Shrin'd in everlasting rest.

Here joyful friend with joyful friend
Meets, and joins the tender kiss:
Endearment grows, no more to end,
High-enhanc'd by conscious Bliss.

And Parents fond their Children dear,
Snatched early to the tomb,
But now matur'd to Saints, meet here,
Shouting joyful—" welcome home !"

Whom Avarice asunder rent,
Cruel Chance or Death controuls,
Embracing Lovers glowing vent
Flames uncheck'd, and mingle Souls.

Heroes contend no more, whose hate
Sunk them to untimely Graves.
Thrown by the idle farce of State,
Tyrants humble to their Slaves.

Bitterest foes, met here at last,
Into warmest friendship grown,
Their little mean resentments past
Quite forget, or blush to own.

Now

Now feel the smarting scourge no more
Negroes, basely bought and sold;
No wretched Captive dreads the oar;
Here no Harpies thirst for gold.

The Poor's no more for meanness scorn'd;
Martyrs here forget the wheel:
All injur'd Innocents, who mourn'd,
Triumph glad on Sion-hill.

The Poor in Fortune, rich in Grace,
Bearing Sorrow, Toil and Pain,
Once righteous in their humble place,
Here in glory Princes reign,

Acclaiming Subjects flock around
Kings, who rul'd with equal sway,
Attesting well, that God has found
Faithful These, as faithful They.

The Brave, the Liberal, the Just,
Truly great and good, content,
Ask no mean honors of a bust,
Grateful Souls their Monument.

To faithful Ministers of Grace,
Praise, peculiar Praise is given;
Saints, whom they sav'd, point as they pass,
" That Man call'd my Soul to Heav'n!"

The

The Bliss imperial of these plains,
(Want whereof wou'd heav'n destroy)
The Bliss of Love eternal reigns;
Love eternal fount of Joy!

One large all-comprehending Love,
Noble, happy, constant flame,
Connects the glorious ranks above,
Saints and Angels, ev'ry Name.

Millions of rival Ardors glow!
Thou adored SOURCE of ALL!
From whom all Beings, Comforts, flow!
Millions at thy footstool fall!

For Love and Gratitude and Awe
Fix all hearts and thoughts on Thee;
Thy glorious Grace, thy righteous Law,
Self-convincing, bend each knee.

O infinite tremendous God!
Whom no Being comprehends!
Eternal Something! at thy Nod,
Nature rises, Nature ends:

On me, a Worm, with grace look down,
Pardon folly, succour toil:
I know, I perish at thy frown,
Gladden at thy pow'rful smile:

The

The Scene, advent'rous Fancy sings,
Impotent, unskill'd, untrue,
May I upborn on seraph-wings,
Rapt to full enjoyment, view!

An ODE.

LET others tune bewitching lays
   To Wine's delights and Beauty's praise,
  Abuse the grape, debauch the fair:
Me, O Urania! still inspire!
Possess my soul with Heav'n's own fire,
  Virtue my passion and my care.

Let learned Lux'ry cater feasts;
'Till human kind be more than beasts
  Enslav'd to Sense by foul excess:
Let me be daily more refin'd
In all the graces of the mind;
  And love all meaner pleasures less.

The magic of luxurious Arts
A while inchants deluded hearts;
  And gay deliriums charm the brain:
But Death or Sickness foils the whole;
And leaves the guilty hopless Soul,
  O'erwhelm'd with horror, shame and pain.

Fix'd

Fix'd in my heart this Thought be still,
Obedience to the sov'reign will
   Alone can happiness secure.
Place Man in Paradise to-day,
If, impious, He will not obey,
   He cannot happy long endure.

Vice, be it natural, if you please;
'Tis Nature's cankering sore disease,
   The bitter source of all our Woe.
To heal this Evil, JESUS dy'd:
O let the thought sink human Pride,
   And bend the stubborn Sinner low!

"*Repent!*" The God of mercy cries:
The Wanton laughs, the Sullen sighs;
   But few repent, reform and turn:
Sweet notes alluring Sin employs;
Inflaming to forbidden joys
   With philtres flowing from her urn.

Smile on *my* suit, indulgent Skies!
" O purge my Reason's dimmed eyes!
   " Unfold your glories to my view!
" Raise my desires mean joys above;
" My bosom fill with holy love,
   " Until I pant alone for you!"

An ODE.

FLY, faithless Visions! Dreams of joy!
　That only charm us to destroy!
Whose painted form and harlot smile
The vicious foolish heart beguile:
The bright conceits, ye glitterers raise,
Fruition evermore betrays.

　Honor and Pleasure, Wealth and Fame,
Which highly human hearts inflame,
Good are ye all, as ye conduce
To social and to civil use;
Good, when possess'd by virtuous men:
'Tis Vice perverts you to be vain:
But, whom ye deign with smiles to bless,
Make ye their wants or wishes less?
Ah no! Like fire each passion grows;
The more the fuel, more it glows;
New cares, new fears, new pains arise;
Not Art and Nature find supplies:
Vain hearts must ake beneath a crown,
And agonize on beds of down!

　The Passions, which enslave the breast,
Are foes to nature, foes to rest:
Far from their empire let me dwell,
Remov'd as far as heav'n from hell.

Give

Give me enough for Nature's needs:
If Heaven's indulgence that exceeds,
As duty, so my heart extends
To all the needy, and my friends.
Give me a calm and chearful mind,
Forever pious, firm and kind:
And let me never play the fool,
As weakly to forget my rule;
Nor place my happiness in state,
In scenes, where love and liquor wait,
In molten ores, in human breath,
Or ought within the reach of Death.

From the Greek of ALPHEUS, *the* MITYLENIAN.

I Wish no large Domain to hold;
  Nor value I the charms of gold.
Content I love, my friend, you see:
Enough is luxury to me.

To JULIUS.

In IMITATION *of the First* EPISTLE *of* BOOK I. *Of* HORACE, 1762.

THOU kind approver of my early strain!
  For Thee is nib'd the long neglected pen.
Indulge the whim, and not the dulness blame;
I never wrote a Candidate for Fame.

Some

Some friendly genius whispers—" *never do!*"
" *When fools enough, what need of Punch and you?*"
So hence away with Rhymes, and Pipe and Lyre:
Truth be my study, Virtue my desire.
Sublimest Views my soaring thoughts employ,
Celestial glory and eternal joy.

Not in his hot nineteenth does Master John
Sigh more for Polly, or for twenty-one;
Not sun-burnt slaves, compel'd with ruthless blows,
Long more for ev'ning cool, and free repose;
No dunce at school, inur'd to whip and scorn,
More ardent wishes for a play-day-morn;
Than I—to know and gain that *best good Thing*,
Of equal benefit to Swain and King;
The which rejecting or neglecting long
Brings equal detriment to old and young.
The fairest light, thank Heav'n! unveiled shines,
The guide and solace of my good designs.

Say, should the blind ophthalmic unguents slight,
Because despairing of an Eagle's sight?
What wretch refuses to expel the Gout,
Because he cannot be as *Sampson* stout?
Health's worth his pains.———Does Av'rice gnaw
    the breast,
Sure, there's a pill to purge the loathsome guest,
                          Bewitch'd

Bewitch'd with glory, there's a charm will ease
The dire enchantment; use it when you please.
For sluggards, drunkards, lovers, there's a balm;
And none so raving, that it cannot calm.
Why, *Thinking*'s all!—Sure, that's no grievous task:
But think with candor: That is all I ask.
Virtue is shunning vice: Wisdom's first Rule
Is nothing more, than, *Do not be a Fool*.
Reflect——what toil and cost a man is at,
To gain a Borough or a large Estate.
The Merchant spreads his sails, to India flies
From want, thro' stormy Seas and burning skies.
Pho! scorn the Trash! Be not so blindly led!
But hear and learn; and trust a better head.
Nay, from the Vulgar learn: Each boxing Blade
Would bruise the *Nailor* *, was he not afraid
Of bruises too; for Honor's something fine
In all degrees; and all aspire to shine.
But mark the prudence!—*Hobson* understood
To want a lesser for a greater good.
Go thou do likewise!——Silver yields to Gold;
And both to Virtue are but dirty mold.

" O Money! precious Money!— That acquire!
" 'Tis honor, pleasure, all you can desire!"

         Thus

---

* A famous Bruiser.

Thus rants each Wit, that plods at Gain and Lofs,
From high St. James's fquare to Radcliffe-Crofs:
This hoary Chuffs to cafh-book Youth inftill:
This edifies the Shopman o'er the till.
Some thoufands more is all *Bob*'s end and pray'r,
That he may fill a feat, or ride Lord May'r:
Adorn'd with all the gentleman, poor Bob,
Without thofe pounds, muft joftle with the mob.
But hear what children fay with better fenfe,
" Be good, my dear! and you fhall be a prince!"
Well fpoke, pure Nature! There the glory lies!
To feel no guilty pangs and blufhes rife!
Does Rofcius, or the children who affign'd
Crowns to the good, think jufteft in thy mind?
Advifes beft the friend, who bids you get,
(And fairly, if you can) a large eftate;
(But yet however) 'till you can appear
Knight of the Shire, or haply rank a Peer;
Or he, who bids you Fortune's flafh deride,
And generoufly fcorn her empty pride?

If Britons afk—"What makes this man not fhare
The common notions, as the common air?"
I tell you, friends! The very fame reply,
Old Reynard made the Lion, that will I.

" The prints all pointing in, and not one out,
" Appear fo ftrangely, I beg leave to doubt."
Stare

Stare not, good people, if I'm not like you:
Whom shou'd I copy! or whose end pursue?
Some thrive by trading; some to play resort;
Some deal in stocks; and others cringe at Court;
All have their turns; the most by humor move;
And hourly vary in dislike and love.

" No place on earth, some Great One says, excels
" *Brightelmston's* healthy coast, and *Tunbridge-
   wells*,"
Smit with the whim, to *Tunbridge-wells* he flies;
Brighthelmston sees the pleasure-boxes rise.
His sickly taste to-morrow takes disgust;
Away packs he to *Bath* with equal lust.
Has Love or Av'rice yok'd him to a wife,
How free and pleasant seems a single life!
If single, then he pants to have a mate;
And swears, *not heav'n excels the nuptial state.*
His happiness where shall we fix? where find?
With what new tie the changing Proteus bind?

What does the poor man?—Laugh?—Yes,
    well you may!
He changes Taphouse, Barber, ev'ry day.
Like richer folk, his fancy quaintly strays;
Dislikes his Lodging, and his hired Chaise.

Suppose

Suppose you meet one shuffling thro' the throng,
Cap'd like old *Monk*, with Cue prodigious long,
Ruff'd to his ears, like a King *Charles*'s shirt,
Dutch-coated too, and sprucely hanger-girt:
You laugh at all this oddity of Dress;
But why?—Is oddity of Temper less?
It loathes, it likes; ne'er with itself agrees;
Conflicts like winds, and rages like the seas.
The case is common:—*Think!*—Don't *laugh* again;
He does not need a doctor and a chain.
We still may laugh or weep, no ease, no end,
If trifles too much tickle or offend.

In short, good Sir, Omnipotence has given
No greater gift than Wisdom under Heaven:
Wisdom is all in one! 'Tis freedom, fame,
And wealth, and ev'ry good, that you can name.

PHYLLIS.

Written 1751, *on the following Thesis,*

Phyllida amo ante alias, nam me discedere flevit,
Et longum formose, Vale, Vale, inquit, Iola.
VIRGIL.

OF all the girls I ever saw
   I love my *Phyllis* best:
Her bosom rivals falling snow,
   In silken scarlet drest.

Her

Her aspect gay, serene and fair
As July's morning sun;
Her easy mien and winning air
Have all my wishes won.

When last we parted in a shade,
The haunt of Philomel,
Oft o'er and o'er she weeping said,
" *Farewel, dear Youth! Farewel!*"

To DORINDA. 1753.

KNEW my DORINDA half how much
    The thought of absence moves me,
Thy Bosom soft, at Pity's touch,
Would melt for him that loves thee.

How long, how deeply, must I mourn,
When years untold deny me
One happy line or blest return;
Since all my stars defy me.

That angel-face, that heav'nly breast
Can I forget?—Ah, never!
O may Felicity still rest!
Where Virtue must forever!

On seeing STELLA.

YE gentle Winds my strains convey,
    And to the Nymph impart,
Whose presence, like the rising day,
Beam's pleasure on my heart.

Since blooming *Stella* brightly shares
Heav'n's glories in her charms,
We well presume she richly bears
Heav'n's blisses in her arms.

O would she deign to be my mate!
With her my fix'd abode
Would make me seem enthron'd in state,
A little Demi-god.

On a SIMILAR INCIDENT.

GUARD, my heart! who is this? like a
    Stranger of Light;
As august as an Angel, as mild and as bright!
See, she looks—all my Face with confusion is
    hung!
Ah, she speaks—but, alas! not a word can my
    Tongue!

I must flee the dear Presence, I long to adore :
Let me dwell in it ever, or see her no more.

To STELLA, 1761.

ODE 7. BOOK III. of HORACE.

WHY, STELLA, flows that stealing Tear?
Anon, the first auspicious gale,
That wafts the Spring, shall spread his sail;
  And faithful *Gyge*, thy belov'd,
In fortune rais'd, in honor prov'd,
  Faithful *Gyge* will be here.

  By furious storms drove o'er the main
In starry Amalthea's reign,
He tastes no joy, nor softly sleeps ;
But thinks on *Stella*, sighs and weeps.

  What tho' some faithless Friend assays
His noble heart ten thousand ways ;
With most devoutly-upcast eyes,
Swears how lovely *Chloe* sighs,
Panting burns, and fainting dies :—

  Perchance relates how *Prætus'* wife
By falsely kindling jealous strife,
Depriv'd the chaste Bellerophon of Life.
                              Relates

Relates what dangers *Peleus* run;
The lewd *Hippolyte* to shun;
Recounts and artfully applies
All stories, countenancing vice:
In vain! Thy *Gyge* still behaves
Firm as rocks, and deaf as waves.

But of thyself, dear Maid, beware!
Thine heart *Enipeus* may ensnare,
Who reins most gracefully the steed,
And cleaves the flood with nimble speed.

Bolt fast the door at dewy Eve;
Let not thy tender ear receive
Those pow'rful notes, which love inspire,
The soft complainings of his Lyre.
To Him, who often cries to Thee,
" Cruel!"—always cruel be!

ODE 9. Book I. of HORACE.

SEE all the mountains white with snow!
  The burthen bends the labouring woods:
The brooks and rills no longer flow;
The north-wind constipates the floods.

Shut

Shut out the cold, and heap the fire;
Freely decant the generous wine,
Which best can pleasantry inspire,
And warm us, till fair weather shine.

Heav'n care the rest!—who soon can lay
The boisterous winds that rowl the Deep;
Still ev'ry breeze, that moves a spray,
And let the shaking Forest sleep.

Pine not about To-morrow: Take
The lot as gain, each day shall bring:
And, ere with palsy'd age you shake,
Ye Youths! be merry, love and sing.

Now is the time for Ball and Play,
And whisper'd tales of love by night:
And now the Wanton, to betray
Her hiding corner, laughs outright;

Struggles, the bracelet or the ring,
In fondness stolen, to detain;
But, for a Kiss, the wished thing,
Resigns it to her darling Swain.

ODE

ODE 12. Book II. of HORACE imitated.

MY Lord, you cannot chuse to hear
    The horrors of a tedious War,
The rough Commanders, and the flood
All red with Carthaginian blood,
    Tun'd to the softly-sounding Lyre:
Neither the savage Party-rage,
Nor slaving* Revels of the Age,
Nor Mobs, that shook th' imperial Throne,
Until by Champions knocked down,
    Do you, my Lord, at all admire.
Yourself in Story best can write
How Roman Troops and Cæsar fight;
What towns they burn'd, what floods they
    crofsd';
How well they won, how well they lost;—
    Yes, You, in bold heroic Song,
Can blazon warlike Glory's scenes;
How sullen Kings and weeping Queens,
And herds of Wretches, drag'd from home
By Heroes, who for mischief roam,
    In Pomp of Triumph stalk along.
Me, humble Me, the Muse bids praise
Your *Lyssy's* sweet inchanting lays:
                           She

---

* Alluding to the Time of a general Election.

She bids me name the Nymph's bright eyes,
And bosom, faithful to your joys:
   The Nymph all virgin-charms adorn:
The easiest Airs, which dancing grace,
The keenest Wit, the finest Face,
The neatest Arm, the best Attire,
Distinguish her among the Choir,
   On great DIANA's festal morn.
Come, tell me truly, cou'd you bear
To lose a lock of *Lyssy's* hair,
For all the Persian Monarch's store,
And all the wealth on Indy's shore,
   When she, with all her winning charms,
Bends her fine neck to let you sip
The neckar'd roses on her lip;
Or else witholds with sweet delay,
What more delights, when forc'd away;
   Or runs herself into your arms?

On SOLITUDE.

O Happy Solitude! I love
   Thy tranquil silence, pensive gloom:
Thought lights her lamp; and from above
Unseen defenders guard the room.

Swift

Swift as a glimpse of light'ning flies
The fire-wing'd Fancy, mental ray;
No space for her too distant lies;
Night's ambient shade is blazing day.

No eye but God's, and Angels blest,
From heav'n commission'd, see and know
Why with extatic joys possest,
Or why dissolv'd in tender woe.

Useless and vain were mean disguise,
Which specious Folly much employs;
An art the Good and Brave despise,
A weapon, which its Lord destroys.

No mirth to make a wise-man sad,
No senseless converse palls the ear;
No Humorist, delicately bad,
No Ruffian, odiously austere.

A conscience calm and clear is ease;
An understanding sound is joy;
Pleasures, which rationally please,
And in fruition never cloy.

God's Works and Word, serene, I scan;
Admire his Wisdom, Justice, Grace;
Or view the busy toil of Man,
The subtil folly of his ways.

Nor

Nor Censure spares myself; but blames
    Ridiculous notions, fond desires:
Conceit degrades, and pride ashames,
    And scorn attends what vice admires.

O Solitude! O calm retreat!
    Both from contempt and flattery free:
That hour, how precious and how sweet,
    With Meditation spent and thee!

An ODE.

THE Morning, like a lovely Bride,
    Sweetly sober, brightly fair,
With decent coyness, modest pride,
    Rising, chears the dewy air.

She comes, Creation's eldest-born,
    Blushing Majesty, she comes;
But now no rose, no blooming thorn
    Breathes upon the wind perfumes.

The sweet returning beam alone
    Gilds this solitary Wild;
While, like a Tyrant from his throne,
    Winter frowns o'er realms despoil'd.

What song, when dreary scenes surround,
  Can the tender Muses sing?
They, soft, with rose and lily crown'd,
  Gratulate the milder spring.

The Muses then alone are gay,
  When the charming Season roves,
Bestrewing flow'rs along her way,
  Circled round with Joys and Loves.

I'll sing of Thee, dread Tyrant, Death!
  Great is thy tremendous pow'r!
Each soul, that lives by mortal breath,
  Aw-struck, waits thy solemn hour.

Vain Confidence at thee, (Heav'n's frown,)
  May, with stupid boldness, laugh;
But at thine arrow drops the crown,
  Coronet and crosier-staff.

The Monarch and the Noble fall
  Prone from Honor's lofty seat:
Thy dreadful quiver levels all
  Empty glories of the Great.

" Kings fall, says Pride, who sit on thrones?
  " Monarchs lie in loathsome graves?"
" Yes, Kings! says Truth, and royal bones
  " Rot, disgrac'd like bones of slaves.

" *Yea,*

" Yea, royal Souls, with all their pride,
   " (Death such change of Fortune brings)
" May *beg* to grace a Peasant's side,
   " Cursing Tyranny in Kings."

The haughty Fury, that o'erwhelms,
   Like the ancient Persian Ram,
Munitions, Mountains, Armies, Realms,
   Will it save? No! deeply damn!

O Pride! thy hateful Works behold!
   Mourn the hideous ruin! mourn!
Hear o'er thy head fierce thunders roll'd!
   See the flames of Vengeance burn!

What's Glory sought by wicked ways?
   Sure a most ridiculous claim!
Wild meteor, self consuming blaze!
   Dies in darkness! sinks in shame!

Pride! Author dire of human woe!
   What from thee, but guilt and pain,
Or did, or could, or e'er can flow?
   Go, thou object of disdain!

Come, Charity! celestial flame!
   Mild as Heav'n, all charming rise!
Sweet harmony of Nature's frame!
   Happiness of happy skies!

What Pow'r divinely shews, like thee,
    Radiant in the human breast?
No other can, besides, agree
    Both to bless and to be bless'd.

Inviolate had'st thou but still
    Reign'd among the sons of men,
None had infring'd the sovereign Will;
    Death had not appal'd us then.

Now since, by Nature's fatal law,
    Scarce thou beam'st on Mortal born,
Let Mercy's clause thy light bestow,
    And relume my waned horn.

By thy pure light relum'd, I'll shine,
    Raised from the gloomy dust,
A Star of righteousness, divine,
    Spher'd in glory 'mong the Just.

Thy graces, Charity, bestow!
    Happiness thro' thee is given:
Thou solely mak'st us blest below,
    Solely mak'st us blest in heav'n.

Thrice happy, happy, who with thee
    Lighted pass this tearful Vale:
Thrice happier, happier, crown'd, who see
    GOD, and in his glory dwell.

An EPITAPH.

SOUL immortal! shun the snares,
   Empty joys and fruitless cares:
Love, and be belov'd of, God;
Use his blessing, use his rod:
Virtue here alone is wealth;
Jesus here alone is health.

ANOTHER.

Suavitas Vitæ! generosa Virtus!
Nec diem summum metuit, nec optat:
Hìc eam cingunt Charites, & inde
                     Gloria Cæli.

EPITAPHS

On four Children, who dy'd of a MALIGNANT FEVER.

I.

THE fiercely-burning flame of Death
   Consum'd our vitals, chok'd our breath;
Yet only did our souls refine,
And fit for endless life divine.

II.

God saw our state, and thought it best
To take us early into rest.
Our lives on Earth were short, to be
The longer in Felicity.

III.

Death is the earthly fate of all:
The Earth itself at last shall fall:
But our Redeemer will restore
To life, in Heav'n, for evermore.

IV.

When the Archangel's trump shall sound,
And wake the sleeping dust around,
Transported We shall wake, and sing
HOSANNA, *to the heav'nly King.*

An ODE.

WHILE yet the breeze diffuses round
    Chilling ruin from its wing,
See, yonder Snow-drop paints the ground,
Beauteous harbinger of spring!

>   Open-bosom'd to the dawn,
>   Fairer than the fairest lawn,
>   Pleas'd and grateful seems to say,
>   " Welcome shine, thou genial Ray !"

Know, pretty Innocent ! how soon
All thy early pride may fly ;
Crop'd by some wanton hand ere noon,
Thou, for cruel nonce, may'st die.

>   Little Venturer ! why steal forth
>   From the lap of matron Earth,
>   All alone in such a Wild,
>   Weak to insults of a Child ?

Hark, how the feather'd Rovers too,
Taught by nature, utter joy ;
The Black-birds whistle, Stock-doves coo :
All their tongues does Love emyloy.

>   Infant lisping Love, who reigns
>   Fondled Tyrant o'er the plains,
>   O'er the Swain and o'er the King ;—
>   Little Love charms all to sing !

Ah, dost Thou know, sweet gentle Dove !
His delight in guile and strife ?

The false ungrateful Serpent, Love,
Stings the breast which gives him life.

  Placid Ease thy bosom fled,
  Anxious thoughts possess instead;
  Milder tho' his looks than thine,
  Cruel is his sly design.

The Knave intends Thee with a mate
To sit moping in a cage,
A wretched prisoner of state,
Till consum'd with spleen and age,

  Conversant with homely cares,
  Dubious hopes and aking fears.
  Shun, ah shun his subtile wiles!
  Trust not his fallacious smiles!

A SONG.

Come, Muse, the lone minutes beguiling!
 Thy Votary calls, come away!
The Loves and the Graces, still smiling,
Prevail and awaken the lay.

 Ye Fair, what's to You more concerning!
Than love, your chief bliss or worst bane?

          'Tis

'Tis friendly to offer you warning;
How love to indulge and restrain.

 Tho' curious your passion, Ah never
Too rashly experience the Wife;
A risque to be happy forever;
Or chain'd to a gally for life.

 Nor, when a fair offer engages,
The crisis of Fortune delay:
One moment may forfeit, what ages
Of anguish and tears can't repay.

 For pride of tormenting Implorers
Defer not the hour to be blest:
The joy of ten thousand Adorers,
And more, in *one* Friend is possest.

 The Rake from his nightly debauches
Comes reeking and staring and pale;
Now lowly, now saucy approaches,
To whisper some fine silly Tale.

 See scribbled, each pane and each leaf on,
Your name and the boast of your charms:
" O pity, dear Lovely!" cries *Strephon*,
And tenderly pants for your arms.

Shall

Shall *this* be the noon of your glory?
If ye to confent be unwife,
Such Fools, who as Gods did adore ye,
Will foremoft deride and defpife.

Difcretely felecting a Suiter,
Forget not the pleafures, that laft:
What torment to bear for the future
Sad fears,—and remorfe for the paft?

The Mifer (fond wretch) coffers money
For thanklefs extravagant Heirs;
The pretty brifk Bee gathers honey
For murdering Ruftics and Bears:

Not fo, ye dear Rofes of Nature!
Your charms fhould be fquander'd away!
If one muft chufe either, 'twere better
With age, unenjoy'd, to decay.

Thofe delicate bofoms and faces
No forrow fhould ever intrude;
Then give not your loves and your graces
To men undifcerning and rude.

The

The MAY.

NOW smiles the MAY: The solar fulgence glows:
The mildest breeze in gentle silence flows.
The banks all painted; spicy blossoms spring:
The sprightly Birds desport on quivering wing;
Or mellow thrill the budding Groves among;
Or glean provision for their callow Young:
While wanton boys with cruel purpose view
The pensile Eyry on the waving bough.

Now *Florimel* the blooming willow shade
Enjoys at Noon, on grassy verdure laid;
On flow'ry pillow, clos'd her pearly eyes,
In happy vision, sweetly smiling, lies.
To humble distance *Colinet* withdraws,
Attends her flock, and guards her calm repose.
Their social flocks, like them united, feed;
Their lambs, like them, sport joyful o'er the mead.
Their tender bosoms, like the Turtle-dove,
Know only peace and innocence and love.
The sweetest herb, the rarest sylvan green
The finest flow'r is in her chaplet seen;
The charming She, the flocks spread o'er the plain,
Content and health o'erjoy the simple Swain.

Now *Agriculture,* beauteous in her youth,
Laughs o'er the fields, triumphing in her growth:
With pleasing hope the peasant views the plain,
The charming promise of his future gain;
Pursues his labor, fill'd with honest joy,
His labor man's original employ;
With useful labor earns what need requires,
Enough for life, and laudable desires;
Sustains the poor, contributes to support
The Public-weal and Glory of the Court.

O happy peasants, delving in the soil!
Whose wealth is vigor, whose amusement toil,
When foes dare injure, bold and strong to wield
Vindictive arms in War's tremendous field,
O if ye knew to prize the boon bestow'd,
Plain Nature's blessings, sweet unenvy'd Good,
The fruits of honest, healthy, chearful toil,
The golden harvest of a grateful soil,
Unknown mean fraud, dissimulation, hate,
And fancy'd cares, which gnaw the soul of State,
Unknown the curses, servile Pride brought forth,
Infernal vipers, torments of the Earth,
Brought forth when languish'd Charity, the tye
Of true perfection, seated in the sky,
The sacred law, whose dictates still incline
The real Happy to a life divine,

Make individuals, self-mov'd, conspire
The general welfare with divine desire;
Then are ye blest! from ev'ry sorrow free,
From ev'ry pang, as human lot can be.

  What curses sprang, when Charity began
At man's apostacy to fail in man?
When Right became constraint instead of choice,
And Laws were made, supplies to Nature's voice?
When Orders rose, some rul'd and some obey'd;
Expedient modes, tho' not by Nature made?
(For Nature's wound, afflicted Reason saw,
Requir'd a cure, and thence devised Law,
Which palliates and repels the prurient sore:
God must extirpate; Reason can no more)
What curses sprang? O if they are unknown
To you, ye swains, your Lot is blest alone.
O, if untaught the proud contempt of Right,
To hate the day, and prowl like Wolves by night;
If, less deprav'd from Nature's perfect plan,
Ye freely hold the Rule becoming Man,
Sincere to moral ties without the awe
Of penal sanctions and coercive law,
How safe, how happy your benignant sphere!
Serenely free from anxious hope and fear!
Rich in true Good, Adversity defy!
Ye reap the Earth, and plant to reap the Sky.

Now *Commerce* hoifts her white expanding fail;
And gayly floats before the founding gale;
Fearlefs of tempefts, that in fury fweep
The rowling furges o'er the roaming deep:
Her precious freight, with Art, her certain guide,
Is fmoothly borne along the heaving tide.
Redundant plenty, curious works of Art,
Whate'er our Soil and Induftry impart,
Commerce tranfports, to blefs thofe diftant lands,
Which *Britain* both enriches and commands;
Or, home-returning, moft profufely pours
All Nature's opulence on *Britain*'s fhores.

Imperial *Britain*! high with Glory crown'd!
O'er all the World for Arts and Arms renown'd!
Pomp gilds thy cities, Plenty glads thy plains,
Sublime Religion, noble Science reigns.
O favor'd Ifle! each high advantage prize;
Deferve diftinction, and by merit rife.
Let Faith and Wifdom on thy pow'r attend;
And be at once the Victor and the Friend.
Purfue the plan, for which all pow'r is given;
And long be thou Vicegerent under Heaven!
A ftorm fometimes awhile obfcures the day;
Heav'n breathes upon it, and it melts away:
So wicked Pow'r, while Heav'n permits, may rage,
The fcourge and terror of an impious Age,
'Till fudden Vengeance ftrike the fatal blow;

Then

Then pomp but ſerves to aggrandize the woe,
Proſper, fair Iſle; and long with joy ſurvey
Delightful ſprings and ſweet returns of May!

Now City-Belles crow'd forth with City-Beaux,
Adorn'd, like Butterflies, in gaudy cloaths;
Friſk o'er the fields, and thro' the meadows range;
The Country breathe, and bleſs the charming change.
Revolting Youth to Love's endearing ſway
Reſign their hearts; and chearfully obey:
Trade's tyrant Pow'r, whoſe ever anxious ſoul
With gloomy rigor does each thought controul,
They now repine: for Nature ſeems poſſeſt;
The genial Joy tranſports each youthful breaſt,
Inſpires reſolves, reluctant to ſuſtain
The dull reſtraint and ſervile care of Gain.
Let, ye ſoft Rovers! vernal ſcenes inſpire
Celeſtial joy, and kindle holy fire.
Reflect whoſe hand the flow'ry carpet lays,
Rears the ſweet groves, and lights yon golden blaze.
Revere his preſence; nor one thought indulge,
One deed aſſay, too ſhameful to promulge.
You, like the plants, his glorious Goodneſs rears;
Fulfils your wiſhes, and averts your fears;
Can always give you what your hearts explore;
Or, that refuſing, grant you ſomething more.

Behold

Behold what Crowds, upon the sacred day,
To worship sacred, but profan'd to play,
What Crowds flock forth! what coaches throng
    the road!
While few lend audience to the word of God.
They view God's works, but a senseless joy;
Receive his gifts, but wantonly employ;
Snatch them unask'd, ungrateful to their friend;
In riot waste, o'erlooking Nature's end.

Or see, where Numbers haunt the House of
    Pray'r
Without devotion; led by Folly there;
Charm'd with the music, or those priests of fame,
Who boldly soar, and pompously declaim;
Their ears admiring the mellifluous tongue,
The pleasant Voice, that tunes a lovely Song.
On Wisdom's charms with extasy they gaze;
Revile her pureness, yet her beauty praise:
She spreads a banquet of eternal Good;
Her bounteous hand extends immortal food:
But vicious hearts refuse her heav'nly fare,
Sweet in the lips, an healing bitter there.
To harlot Folly their desires incline,
Whose golden cup o'erflows with philter'd wine:
Inchanting music fills her myrtle bow'r,
Entwin'd with bayes; and roses strew her floor.
Gay magic Scenes, ideal Splendors, fair
To Fancy's view, but empty all as air,
                         Delude

Delude the guilty Throng with fatal joy,
Allure with smiles, that blandish to destroy.
O shun her snares! the snares of Folly shun!
Keep Virtue's path, as Earth around the Sun
Undevious rolls: that holy Will obey,
Which blesses all, and beautifies the May.

To the SINGING BIRDS.

FREE and merry in each bush
   Warble Nightingale and Thrush:
Crown'd with chaplets, blooming May
Harks delighted to the lay.
Happy, happy, happy Choir!
Sweetest, softest Joys inspire!

   Say what touch on pleasure's springs,
Tunes the voice, expands the wings,
When the sprightly plumy race
Such extatic joys express?

   Reason's foil'd, and Art disgrac'd:
Man may envy, never taste:
'Tis a purer Sense, that brings
More delicious taste of things:
Simple Nature's beauty warms;
Birds are pleas'd with Nature's charms.

Match'd

Match'd with them, my learned friends
Nothing know of Nature's ends,
Nothing act of wife defign,
Juft to ordinance divine.

Never boaft your learned toil,
Thoughtful LOCKE and curious BOYLE!
Birds fagacity can fhew,
LOCKE cou'd not explain nor know.
BOYLE, behold the fipping Bee
Better fkill'd in flow'rs than Thee.

Life to you, ye warblers gay,
All is pleafure, all is play.
Feaft and fong begin with light;
Leafy arbors lodge by night.
Knows the little Bird one forrow?
Cares her heart about To-morrow?

Yes, the Reas'ner, prone to wrong,
Robs her of her callow young.
Ah, furprized from her neft,
Scarce fhe trufts a bough to reft.
Spoil'd by man's rapacious race,
Moaning, fhe forfakes the place.
Ah, Misfortune never knows
Where fhe fafely may repofe!

Blufh

Blush, thou Tyrant of the Ball!
Reas'ning Savage! worst of all!
Why distress, in cruel sport,
These sweet minstrels of thy court?
What infernal joy to make
Nature wretched for thy sake?
Wretched for thy cruel pride,
Curse of all the World beside?

Pretty Birds! your joys pursue!
Hop and chirp from bough to bough,
I, with rapture, when I rove,
Hear the music of the Grove!
Music, sweetly, softly shrill,
Flowing from each polish'd bill;
From among the silken trees,
Trembling on the vernal breeze.
Nothing, Warblers, need ye fear
An admirer so sincere.

Pleas'd am I to tune the Lyre,
Grateful to the plumy Choir.
When they cease their loves and songs,
Cold their hearts and mute their tongues.
When I too am with the Dead,
Let these grateful lays be read,

ODE 30. Of ANACREON.

ONCE the *Muses*, flow'ry-crown'd,
  Cupid in their garlands bound;
Then to *Beauty* gave the Boy.
Venus fought her little Joy.
" *Let the pretty Captive go*,
" *Venus millions will bestow.*"
Go!—not He!—the Boy remains,
All delighted with his chains.

The KISS.

A Wanton Boy, us'd I to stray
  In woods and lawns, where *Dryads* play:
Where'er was mirthful dance and song,
I, wildly joyous, join'd the Throng.

 Then simple I, jocund within,
Saw Paradise in ev'ry scene:
The country bloom'd, the birds were gay;
The flocks were blithsome; all was May.

 Among the *Dryads*, one, most fair,
And most genteel in dress and air,
Still chose me Partner, while the grace
Of smiles and blushes spread her face:
        She

She squeez'd my hand; whereon, I vow,
I squeezed hers and blushed too.
We look, and smile, and blush and sigh,
And hate to part, we know not why.

Sometimes in groves or grots around
She hid, on purpose to be found:
In thickest shade wou'd I surprize
The beauteous Darling of my eyes;
Or, if I long in vain had sought,
She laugh'd aloud, and so was caught.
Sometimes where'er my walking led
She watch'd, and, when she saw me, fled:
She, glad to be o'ertaken, flew;
I, glad to overtake, pursue.

One day, my *Dryad*, sweetly meek,
Most tenderly did pat my cheek;
" *Come, press your Lips to mine,*" she said;
Her fond conceit I soon obey'd:
But, O ye happy Gods! how stole
Inchanting pleasure on my soul?
No spicy flow'r on *Carmel* grows,
No honey-oak near *Hybla* flows,
No nectar springs in your abodes
Half so delicious, O ye Gods!

Again

Again she glu'd her lips to mine:
Intoxication how divine!
" *My dearest Charmer!*" I exclaim'd,
" *Was e'er this wondrous pleasure nam'd,*
" *Which from your lips, when mine they meet,*
" *Glides thro' my very soul so sweet?*
" *What call you the inchanting Bliss?*
She rosy-smil'd, and lisp'd—" A KISS!"

A SONG.

BELIEVE not too fondly, beware, gentle Maids!
Lest turtles prove jays in disguise.
A Lover's a rose in your bosom, that fades;
Neglected, that suddenly dies.

Fix passion with prudence, where reason may still
To friendship and constancy bind;
Where virtue and sense may determine your will,
When raptures remit, to be kind.

Eternally Love's happy bondage endures,
If Prudence her captives detains:
Whatever Charm conquer'd, 'tis Prudence secures
The captive, and rivets his chains.

A SONG.

A SONG.

YE Swains! never wander from honor and truth:
Earn age no remorse with the follies of Youth.
In loving the Fair, he's the truest enjoyer,
Who guards the soft breast from each cruel destroyer.

If any Seducer, infernally nurs'd,
Betrays with endearment, the wretch be accurs'd!
A dæmon, for blasting the glory of Beauty,
And tainting affection to violate duty.

Wou'd you what is amiable love, and be blest,
Spread Virtue's pavilion for Beauty to rest:
Let Prudence Esteem and Affection attend her;
And Constancy comfort, support and defend her.

Nor think from mere Beauty long joy can accrue.
The pluck'd blossom fades; admiration palls too.
'Tis goodness is ever (who want it may railly)
The jewel of principal lustre and value.

A Novice, enamor'd of vain Beauty's smile,
In extasy views the fine statue awhile;
But Constancy lives on the permanent graces
Of minds more adorned and charming than faces.

A SONG.

A SONG.

SAY, can Natures discordant complacency know?
Can the Fox with the Lamb, or the Wolf with
    the Roe?
Can the Jay with the Linnet, the Hawk with the
    Dove?
Then may tempers ill-suited be happy in love,
Then be wise, youthful Lovers, in choosing for life,
Both Phebe her husband, and Colin his wife.

Ne'er dissemble affection, delude with a shew;
And industriously lay the foundation of woe?
All the Mischievous merit the mischief, they meet:
No convention is sacred with hostile Deceit.
So in love as in life, the old proverb is true,
To be honest—and then honest dealing's your due.

Know that Virtue alone can be happy; for still,
There's no evil so fatal, so pregnant, as Will.
Let your principal object be merit: you'll own,
'Tis a folly to hope for a crop never sown.
Let your own cultivation the blessing refine;
And deserve the affection of, who deserves thine.

The WALNUT TREE;
An ELEGY.
Written at the Request of a Lady.

WHAT *Muse* is deaf to gentle *Beauty*'s call;
    Or stands insensible at *Friendship*'s voice?
The *Muse* obeys: *To sing the Walnut's Fall*,
Pleasing command! obedience is but choice.

Your silver harps, ye sylvan *Fairies*, bring,
Which guide your dances by the silent Moon:
To plaintive song wake each immortal string;
The mournful Theme demands a mournful Tune.

Fair *Walnut-tree*, ye fairy Choir, there stood
In Garden green, on gently-rising hill,
A little blooming Sister of the Wood,
Where Thrush and Blackbird, shady, sung at will.

But late (Alas! what merit e'er was found
To save, when higher Pow'rs our fall decree)
The Owner fancy'd she incumber'd ground—
" Gard'ner! dig up this useless *Walnut-tree*."

The sentence past, intreaties all are vain;
Her vital roots dismantled soon appear:
And *Dick* and *Tom*, with sturdy might and main,
Mangled and lopp'd; no enemy, no fear!

The Poet, to complete her overthrow,
Climb'd up, and bound with rope her leafy boughs:
Ah, cruel Poet! justly to thy woe!
For thou, in climbing, sore thy shins did'st bruise.

Then from his Tent, in leathern armour, came
Stately Bucephalus*, and seiz'd her bound;
He, strongly tugging, stretch'd his brawny frame,
And brought poor *Walnut* tumbling to the ground.

The sorrowing *Dryads* trembled when she fell!
Untimely fell! her fruits were premature!
Lament, ye *Fairies! Echo*, from thy cell,
Lament poor *Walnut*'s—*Walnut*'s dying hour!

What guilt of thine provok'd unpitying Fate?
What excellence offended Envy's eye?

Not

---

* *A Coach Horse.*

Not humble innocence protracts thy date:
See! like the Great and Honor'd, see her die!

Exempt is no condition from decay;
No Lord nor Shrub on earth from Death is free:
What profit then of all this World have they?
Why Fame!—And Fame's a Walnut-elegy.

Your harps, ye *Fairies*! this last boon demands;
Her fate untimely solemnly deplore!
That done, your harps unstrung with trembling hands
Hang on the Willows—*Walnut* is no more!

To A YOUNG LADY.

A Leisure hour, an indolent repose,
   No pastime here, but what from Fancy flows;
A mind too dull to think, too brisk to rest,
Drive me to plague some friend; I choose a Best.
Strange humor mine!—*I ever scorn to teaze
A silly Wretch, whom I disdain to please.*

"*Why*

"*Why write to me?*" you cry: "What have
    I done,
"To bear your nonsense?—Friendship! when
    begun?"

Nay, own *you know me:* Surely that's all one!
With many folks *'tis friendship to be known.*
Vain I may be: impertinent, 'tis true;
But then my folly cannot injure you.

"*Yes! teaze me!*"—Well! but, at so cheap
    a rate,
Will not your goodness ease a Noodle's pate?
For write I must!—In songs my ink may flow;
Songs of my own: Fine *Strephon's* are not so.
Many prefer the Nightingale's wild note
To what Canary trills thro' artful throat.
Perhaps I moralize, not blush to give
Advice, where it becomes me to receive:
That matters not! for that's our common way;
Archbishops hear what Curates have to say.

"It ill becomes ye then to make too free:
"Low brazen fellows! prating! what are ye?"

Why, Madam! if appearances wo'd pass,
The Lion might be frighten'd at the Ass.
Nor can we always judge of right and fit:
A licence too is claim'd by *Men of Wit.*

        F   "Do

"Do you claim *that* ?"—Well, now I own,
    I blush:
The solid proof is wanting at the push:
Nothing to shew!—However, when you please,
Bid me depart—I vanish—You're at ease.
Read my impertinence, or burn, or tear;
Wrap up your thread in't, or curl up your hair:
'Tis good for something!—And remember still,
We often for the Deed shou'd take the Will.

To the Same. On Reading.

CUSTOM with Folly seems in *this* combin'd
    Against you females—*To immure the Mind*;
As if much knowledge made the morals worse;
Heav'n's choicest blessings were the greatest curse.
My vote concurs to cut all slavish reins;
And bind in Duty's softer, stronger, chains.
What! treat the *Fair,* as popish Priests their
    flocks!
Like injur'd Negroes! like a muzzled Ox!
Undue restraints are brambles of distress
In Virtue's path, provoking to transgress.
Heav'n leaves us free: To move us to obey,
Reveals high grace, delineates the way.
This god-like plan the Generous will pursue.

All

All true obedience springs from knowledge true,
Presumptuous Folly still its end defeats:
Deceivers perish by their own deceits.
They, who presume the female soul design'd
For no great purpose of a reas'ning mind,
Allow those studies, which the mind debase,
As if in spite, to compass its disgrace.
" Tales and Romances for a Lady's ear!"
Sublimer studies too sublime appear.
Ladies must only learn the loves of Rakes,
'Till Virtue nods asleep and Vice awakes.
Hence infant hearts pant with the pleasing flame,
Which flashes, darts and glows through all the
      Frame,
Almost ere words are found to give it name.
Admit Romancers write in Virtue's cause;
Through ev'ry page a subtile poison flows:
The fatal fomes kindles curious thought,
'Till all the soul is into tumult brought.
Passions to anarchy resistless rise;
And Prudence, vanquish'd, in the riot dies.

  " They learn the world this way!" Perhaps
      they do:
They learn its vices and its follies too;
Without the previous skill, that task requires;
To know such objects, free from such desires.

                      I own,

I own, such reading greatly may conduce,
Well-tim'd, well-temper'd, to the Reader's use;
Quell in the closet Passion's Reasons's strife;
And send her warn'd, prepared, into life:
Yet still, such books demand, whenever read,
The coolest heart, or most experienc'd head:
For Passion, in the violent and young,
Will make the Vice seem right, the Virtue wrong;
Or not discern the Author's good designs,
Which oft might be compriz'd in two short lines.

The grand intent's t'unravel mazy man;
And set a guard o'er Beauty, if they can;
Shew whom you love, are dæmons in disguise;
And that in pride and art your safety lies.
O sad resource! O shameful truth to tell!
O spoil of sin! how low is nature fell!

Your pardon, Madam!—'Tis perhaps too hard
To hint, your prudence e'er can need a guard.
Indeed I blush for my officious pen!
You know, you shun, you hate base-hearted men.
Saw you a Fool since life's first pulse did leap,
But that affected *to be sly and deep?*
Brand such a Wretch for Fool, howe'er he blaze;
He really is weak, as well as base.

Mean Cunning ever is an empty boaſt:
Miſchievous Wits outwit themſelves the moſt:
Their triumphs are the doting of an hour,
Unleſs upheld a while by wealth and pow'r.
Friends muſt as Foes the wretches mean deſpiſe,
Who, blind to Good, are only damn'dly wiſe:
Their guile, ſo odious ſcarce can be forgiven
By God or Man; accurs'd by Earth and Heav'n.
But poor's the ſolace to a Maid undone,
To think, his doom her ſpoiler cannot ſhun.

Another evil oft bad Reading brings;
It makes nice Critics in ridiculous things;
Taints Folly's boſom with a large ſupply
Of falſe ſenſations—Lord knows what, and why!
Mere phantom-objects all the mind employ;
Give half its pains, ſpoil more than half its joy;
Render uneaſy, when no harm is near,
Except its own weak whim, and ſilly fear.
The Being, thus abas'd appears as frail,
And ſorely tender, as a pappy ſnail;
Shrinks with fantaſtic peeviſhneſs or dread;
Acting the Ideot,—to be ſure fine bred!
Fit but to languiſh in a downy chair,
A Fop, a Pug and Parrot all her care.

The Reading I wou'd humbly recommend,
Nor quite reject the other in the end,
Is history, civil, natural, great and small;
Divinity, the grand concern of all;
Moral productions; the chaste Muse's lays;
(Instructions she most charmingly conveys)
Why shou'd philosophy be deem'd too high
For beings so near related to the sky?
All Books, that tend t' ennoble and refine,
Ladies may read:—Let such, my Fair! be thine.

To the same. On HABIT.

SOULS after death, as certain Ancients say,
Inform anew some organized clay:
Brutes transmigrate to Men, and Men to Brutes;
Assuming each the kind, which fancy suits.
If this be true (for all's not true, that's said)
This World, ye Fair! is then a Masquerade.
Well, so be it!—You'll grant the sages this,
The fancy's pretty, and not much amiss.

One time, an Edict pass'd, as story goes,
For each to name the fashion, which he chose;
And Mrs. *Lachesis* (she, Ma'm, you'll guess)
Was Pattern-maker for the masquing dress)

Produc'd

Produc'd her patterns of each kind and form,
From man imperial to the crawling worm.
Amid the throng one old *Therſites* came,
Since Troy's cataſtrophe well known to fame;
Known for malicious jibes and ſpiteful tricks;
A viler ghoſt ne'er preſs'd thy waves, O Styx!
When his turn came to chooſe an earthly ſhape,
The queer old Soul with joy ſelects an Ape.
" His choice ſeems odd!"--At firſt perhaps it may;
But the ſame fault is acted every day.

    The God of Nature wondrouſly aſſign'd
A *Turn* peculiar to each human mind:
That each an end peculiar may purſue,
Men's humors differ more than faces do:
If join'd with Virtue, all theſe *Turns* produce
Peculiar acts of private public uſe.
That all, made free, fit uſes might maintain,
God bade right Reaſon his Vicegerent reign.
But things, the nobleſt in their firſt deſign,
Become the baſeſt, tending to decline:
The cordial grape, abus'd by wrong degrees,
Induces dulneſs, anguiſh and diſeaſe:
Things all, which uſed well moſt ſweet impart,
Spoil'd by exceſs, excite the keeneſt ſmart:
Prime Angels, exil'd from celeſtial light,
Are felleſt Dæmons in tartarean night:

                        Thus

Thus that peculiar *Turn*, by gracious Heaven
To ev'ry soul for noble uses given,
Deprav'd with Vice, with passions base and blind,
Becomes the great distemper of the mind:
Indulg'd to Habit, makes mankind appear
Like beasts; and various as brute species are.

If ruling Reason only reigns a drone;
Or weakly yields, and abdicates her throne;
The Passions deviate to what we condemn;
And ev'ry choice is monstrous, made by them.
Hence some embrace, with ravenous delight,
What Reason shuns with laughter or affright:
Some sink below their kind, below the beast;
Greatest in mischief, as in goodness least:
No light, no law directs the phrenzy'd soul;
The body is a Bedlam, dark and foul.

Thus all the Passions into Vice may go;
And, if indulg'd, to vicious Habit grow.
Habit grows stubborn soon, since always join'd,
And woven with the native *Turn* of mind:
Age so confirms it in th' immortal frame
It braves all fortunes, and is still the same.

Hence

Hence, in all stations,* under ev'ry shape,
Thersites' Soul delights to act the Ape.

His coarse example warns us to controul
Those giant Passions, that convulse the Soul;
Lest those, unbridled, brutally deface
The Maker's Image and the works of Grace:
It bids us shun ill Habit, as a scar,
An hectic fever, or an hoiden air;
All very odious to the gentle Fair;
And for this reason worse to be endur'd,
Because by time and judgment hardly cur'd.

---

* It may be doubted whether ill Habits, respecting particular objects, do remain in a future State, where those objects are not found: but still such Habits are equally pernicious; for they destroy that virtue firmness, purity and health of Soul, which alone can render it, in any state, morally good and perfectly happy. And who knows whether the desire, as well as remembrance, of things past will not, in some sort, revive in a future State? Several Heathens and Christian Fathers assert, that Souls unbody'd are invested with certain material vehicles (Αὐγοειδὲς or Spectres) in which they (or at least, the bad sort of them) do retain some capacity for sensual Pleasure and Pain. This, among other ancient Notions, is now commonly exploded; but we shall probably greatly err, if we think all that is exploded is comtemptible.

See *Origen.* Contra *Celsum.* Lib. II. also the parable of Dives and Lazarus.

The MIND.

GO look thro' Art and Nature, you shall find,
   The greatest wonder is the human *Mind*.
Its fair imperial excellencies shew
Man's title to Supremacy below:
Yet so absurd its Wisdom, mean its Pride,
Nothing is so ridiculous beside.

  Much boasted wisdom, long and hardly sought,
Is only noise, futility, stark nought.
They, who the heights of Metaphysics soar,
Bring down some truths, but idle guesses more.
They, who thro' Nature's dark abysses roam,
Often return, like other Travellers, home;
Spoil common-sense, and impudently scorn
All those high ends, for which Mankind are born.

  Could each inspect his neighbor, as he sees
Thro' crystal walls a factory of Bees;
Then might he view the brisk ideas run,
Like Insects dancing in the ev'ning sun;
Their kinds and numbers; how they rise and join;
What counsels form; with what desires combine.

'Tis my conjecture—(and with reason too)
That, while this strange phaenomenon were new,
Ere we discern'd Ideas range by rule,
The wisest would appear the greatest fool;
And humbler minds, which fewer scenes produce,
Seem most consistent, and compos'd for use.
So yonder stars appear to vulgar eyes
Strewn very carelesly about the skies;
Devoid of regular and wise design;
Stamp'd with no signatures of skill divine:
Your Connoiseurs judiciously prefer
A bronze, a picture, or a poor parterre:
The reason's plain—because they comprehend
A trivial System, and the Author's end.

Could we the thoughts of busy mortals view;
Their wisdom, happiness; their good and true;
Then might we see on what nice springs depends
The spite of Foes, the tuneful love of Friends;
Why oft unmeaning sounds deceive our ears;
Why Ignorance in Learning's garb appears:
Might trace the curious plan of Wisdom's thought;
And Folly's cobwebs in each corner wrought.

What pretty fabrics Sophisters could shew,
Little inferior to a fort of straw?
Finite prov'd infinite with dext'rous art;
And that the whole's no bigger than a part;

What

What source supplies the Sun's exub'rant flame;
What pow'r mechanic moves the Mundane frame;
How Souls commence by Motion's natural rule;
And chief—Man's privilege to be a Fool.

What engines would the Statesman's soul reveal!
Most like the Prophet's Vision, wheel in wheel:
Stores of ingenious levers, screws and springs,
To manage Mobs and Patriots and Kings:
Arrangements such, that still 'tis understood,
The Statesman's private, must be public, good.

The Poet's brain great wonders would unfold;
The art occult, base metals turn'd to gold:
Each country Village by its magic seem
Elysium; and each Brook, Pactolus' stream.
If wanton Love the soft design inspire,
To make fair bosoms heave with fond desire;
Then might you see compos'd the mellow song,
That warbles phrenzy thro' the list'ning throng.
Should Satire fell in venom dip his pen,
In Virtue's cause to blast unrighteous men;
With more than hydra-heads, and killing eyes
Of Basilisk, his armed Rage will rise.
Should Grace divine her sacred warmth impart;
To stir the brisk vibrations of his heart;
Then would he charm you with an holy zeal,
Far more than *Orpheus* teaching rocks to feel.

The Beau—methinks I have him in my eye;
And see how all his little toy-things lie.
His own dear Image first at length appears,
By Mode, his Valet, trim'd from toes to ears:
Next to his quaint fantastic stupid Mien
Lies baby Speech, and Fondness to be seen;
Courtship to ev'ry eye-ball to admire;
Hope, that the Ladies will—in vain—desire.

The Hypocrite, secure in blind applause,
With lying phiz and sanctimonious saws,
Would shew a scene (Heav'n save us!) shocking
    sight!
A miniature of Satan rob'd in light.

Within the Miser we should see those fears,
Which keep unclos'd his eyes, arrect his ears;
Where ne'er a noble sentiment can glow,
Nor mild compassion, anodyne for woe!
His prone poor soul still poring on the clod,
Pining in plenty and blaspheming God.

The Libertine—what pencil can describe!
Whether of brutal or infernal Tribe
Let Naturalists resolve:—But of the two
A mongrel progeny would I allow,
To rail on heav'n, to riot on the earth;
The shame of Her, who gave the Monster birth:

                           Professed

Profeſſed foe to Nature, Life and Soul;
No Tears can ſoften, as no Ties controul.
Could thought be ſeen in him, how loath'd a
 crew
Of foul Ideas would pollute the view!

What would I ſay?—The winged Moments fly,
To waft the hour, when ev'ry form muſt die,
Thoughts all revive, and naked ſtand the gaze
Of Earth and Heav'n in God's expoſing blaze:
At that Tribunal even *this* may riſe,
Or to acquit or to condemn J—. WISE.

To two LADIES, *who pleaſantly chid the* AUTHOR
for an involuntary DISAPPOINTMENT.
July 26. 1764.

LADIES, permit confeſſion to atone!
 This ſeeming error really was none.
I own myſelf for non-attendance ſham'd:
Wilful omiſſion juſtly might be blam'd.
Put *that* the caſe, the argument would be,
Neglect of you implies defect in me;
Want of diſcernment—and a want that's worſe!
One fault includes a dozen more, of courſe.
But *that* the caſe was not:—The cauſe was great!
To dire neceſſity muſt all ſubmit!

If

If ill appearances my plea oppose,
And cast I am by over-rigid Laws;
Forgive him once, who needs it often;—give
Your mild reprieve; and let your Convict live.
Not worth in me, but grace in you, I plead.
'Tis your own cause!—I'm penitent indeed!
Did *Shakespear*'s Nature, *Pope*'s fine Art inspire
Your Poet's numbers with energic fire;
Full in your ears the piercing notes should roll,
To mollify and charm the list'ning soul.
Did *Richardson*'s most gentle spirit breathe,
Ordain'd to wear Fame's everlasting wreath,
Whose pathos strong and language finely free
Sieze all the heart (a conquest own'd by me!)
Oe'r which, while merit charms a British eye,
Bright orbs shall weep, and fairest bosoms sigh;
Breath'd his blest spirit, then should periods flow!
Prose, soft as air, and pure as falling snow!
Hearts, not like yours—ev'n hearts ally'd to stone
Should melt to read, and tender mercy own.
But I, alas! no such advantage find;
My fancy feeble, and my judgment blind:
So poor a pleader, in the justest cause,
Must go content with pity for applause.

Your various *Graces* when I number o'er,
I feel your worth and my presumption more.

Celestial

Celeſtial BOUNTY, at the deſtin'd hour,
Sent down her Angels with peculiar pow'r.
Beauty fine tints, and waxen forms, with care
Compos'd and finiſh'd; nor forgot one hair.
Had he beheld the workmanſhip ſupreme,
Narciſſus had eſcap'd the fatal ſtream.
Painting beſtows the pencil's nice command,
Ten-times more charming in a charming hand.
Officious *Muſic* needleſs aid imparts;
Ah, one's enough t' enchant a million hearts!
BOUNTY was laviſh in that hour; for ſtill,
Wit points thoſe charms, and gives them pow'r to
    kill.
Nay, BOUNTY had been cruel ſo to do,
But that ſhe join'd *Benevolency* too.

Invidious *Graces*! Why do ye combine
To ſhew my dimneſs, as the more ye ſhine?
Yet while I view, I feel (and thence am bleſt)
Something cogenial animate my breaſt.
Blaze, 'till, refin'd by your indulgent ray,
Like you I ſhine, and blend a mutual day.

But how can I, at humble diſtance caſt,
Look up to you, whoſe very frown would blaſt;
'Leſs you in goodneſs graciouſly reſtore,
At leaſt, the ſun-ſhine, you indulg'd before?

                            With

With different tempers diff'rent treatment suits:
This truth shall be exemplify'd in brutes.

A pamper'd *Spaniel*, over dainty grown,
Disdains to fetch and carry for a bone;
Sneaks off, and tries his miscreant head to hide,
Conscious of guilt and cowardly in his pride;
But, if you discipline his sides with cane,
The Culprit's your obsequious Slave again;
Creeps to your feet, and fawns with so much sense,
As if he'd rather die, than give offence.
Submission charms us: We are born to rule:
But i'n't the Dog a rascal and a fool?
The *Lap-dog*, conscious, not of worth possest,
But of strange fondness in his Lady's breast,
Now sooths, now snarls; not fearing to offend;
Meanly ungrateful to his too-kind Friend;
From base ill-humor ne'er is he exempt,
Except when school'd by hunger and contempt.
The favor'd *Lion*, of a noble mind,
Is grateful without meanness; firmly kind,
But servile never: We must still approve
His generous spirit, in resent or love.
Honor *will* always, and alone *can*, draw
His noble soul; for Honor is his law.

These *Turns* of diff'rent beasts (and more by ten)
May all be found in our one species men:
Nay, Fiend and Angel scarce more distant are,
Than man from man, in point of Character.

A Tale so plain, 'twere folly to apply:
You know the moral better much than I:
With nice discernment to inspect the mind,
And treat with just distinction ev'ry kind.

So far as it concerns myself, I'll say:
Great Nature formed Me of pliant clay:
Own your admirer, set his heart at ease,
He's this or that, whate'er your Graces please.

To a LADY.

'TWAS when this *Globe*, where, destin'd, we to-day
Enjoy the feast, the labor and the play,
To hate to love, to sorrow and to laugh,
To follow feathers, fight for nature's chaff—
'T when, I say, this Globe, this earth and main,
Turn'd this side from the *Sun*, to turn again;

As

As men repent, to sin with keener taste;
Or change their follies, sated with the past:
The *Sun*, remote, just left *Britannia*'s eyes;
While *Evening* stay'd behind to close the skies:
The *Sun*'s old porter, like a noble, stood;
His gaudy livery was a suit of cloud,
Flowing down gracefully in many a fold,
Sable and crimson, edg'd with beamy gold:
'Twas then, when *Belles*, who hate the rude-ey'd
  Sun,
Which broadly stares, and looks their beauties
  dun,
When *Belles*, most like gay Goddesses, at eve,
Steal forth to breathe, and votive sighs receive,
Guarded with bipeds, vulgarly call'd *Beaux*,
Human in form, but something more in cloaths,
Larger than lap-dogs, timid yet as those;
'Twas then, I say, at that important hour,
When Love and Beauty rule in height of pow'r,
That I, from their dominion long ago
Condemn'd an exile, yet esteem'd no foe,
Immur'd in solitude, and musing o'er
The various incidents of life before,
Rose, as did Sampson from th' insidious bed,
Snapping his fetters like a sindged thread;
I, from reveries rising, did divest
The bonds of *Indolence*, my treacherous guest;
Aim'd to be chearful, tho' too dull to jest:

        My

My idle hand fnatch'd up the ready pen,
Refolv'd to fcrawl to You, juft there and then.

How happy to augment, tho' but a mite,
The facred treafury of your delight!
Each fool can injure, and each fop can teaze;
The friendly *Mufe* afpires to aid and pleafe;
And, to thofe ends, is curious to purfue
Some object, worthy her, and worthy you.

Faint is the pleafure, and too frail t'endure,
Which rhymes, like mine, ignoble, can procure;
But (thanks to Heav'n!) you hold the fureft
    claim
To nobleft pleafures, pleafures fcorning fame:
Worth is the title, which your claim can raife;
Confefs'd by all, from whom one values praife:
Free adoration meets her glorious beam;
While crowns and kingdoms cannot buy efteem.

The Great may flutter in the gorgeous fpoil
Of land and fea; and quaff the fweets of toil;
Stride o'er the world, our envy and our fear;
Seem drunk with joy; but *Worth* is joy fincere!
Serenely fhining, like the fixed pole
Immoveable, immortal as the foul.
Sometimes a cloud conceals her from our fight;
But feen, we gladly celebrate her light.

                              When

When Friendship, like a mist-dispelling gale
At summer's morn, develops once the veil,
The veil of modesty, which her confines,
We see transported, and exclaim--*She shines!*

Indeed but few are just to what they feel:
The chains of Form, more strong than chains of
    steel,
Tie mute the friendly tongue; or foppish Art,
Sounding her praises, overtops its part,
And breeds disgust; or Envy (constant shade)
Clouds her with slander, 'till she seem to fade.
Such is the fate, that Worth must ever find
Among all ranks of Vulgar in mankind.

Great God of Heav'n and this terraqueous
    ball!
Who giv'st, rejoicest in, the good of all;
Who feest the heart, who ev'ry thought dost
    weigh!
Who honor'st truth, and them who truth obey!
How dares the heart assume perverse disguise?
Is to dissemble or calumniate wise?
Rather be truth beyond all human reach,
Than so disgrac'd by ill-according speech:
Nay, man be dumb!--why should set Heav'n
    refuse
What man will either stifle or abuse?
                            My

My voice shall ever boldly trumpet forth,
Wherever due, the just applause of Worth!

Pope, whom you read, in principle was free;
His art, not doctrine, is admir'd by me:
Too superficial on a theme profound;
His maxims false, his arguments unfound:
Blindly astray in metaphysic road,
He charges Evil all on Fate and God:
But yet, he could not fairly Sin acquit:
Let us, where due, lay all the blame, on *it*.

Attach'd to pleasure, and of genius vain,
Many forge systems in their airy brain;
Nature and God to their strange fancies bend,
Explaining Both to suit their fav'rite end;
To suit licentious appetite and pride;
And set the rigid Scripture-truths aside:
(For, since the precepts on the faith will stand,
The Creed must fall, to murder the Command)
But surely 'tis a wretched course, they take,
Who strive to be perswaded to mistake:
A false perswasion can but lull their fear
A little space, to let them riot here:
The Fiends of Death will shortly sieze them prey,
And drag to torments, deep-immur'd from day.

O why

O why do Sinners hate the Scripture-creed,
Where Grace invites? 'Tis, sure, what *they* most need!
On Nature's law presume they to rely?
They still choose bane! by Nature's law they die.
Stern Nature thunders -" Die!"--without reprieve:
Mild Grace alone calls sweetly—" Turn and live!"
Repentance, true, (hard task!) she claims: she must!
She can but save *the willing to be just*.
Sacred thro' Christ, does her commission run;
Such honor God decrees himself and son,
The *Holy Ghost* must have due homage paid,
Christ's Vicar sent with Angel-hosts, our aid.
Ah! wou'd we less?—Shou'd Majesty divine
His most illustrious attribute resign,
His peerless Holiness? Nor rise to prove
Of Sin his hate, of Righteousness his love?
No! Truth forbids!—To all he'll have it known,
None without holiness approach his Throne.
In *Christ* he means this lesson to display;
Then bids—*All him embrace, All him obey.*
Whoe'er this sacred Name perversly spurn,
Though crown'd in this World, in the next shall
   burn:
Whoe'er this sacred Name aright revere
Shall shine in Glory there, tho' abject here.

This

This World, dear Lady, (*Dear* let me addrefs!
Word never pen more juftly might exprefs)
This World's a jeft: regard the World to come.
Our conduct here decides our future doom.
Act the immortal!—Short, unfure the date,
Frail each condition, of this mortal State,
Why fhou'd its higheft joys engrofs our care;
Or deepeft woes o'erwhelm us with defpair?
Why fhou'd they tempt us out of Virtue's road,
To rifque our title to the grace of God?
Adhere to truth; and then your claim is fure,
And then alone, to joys, which fhall endure.

But, left my Friend fhou'd think, I cenfure hard;
And with injurious fcorn condemn her Bard;
I own his numbers rife with accent true;
And fall with cadence foft as morning dew:
Good fenfe and wit, to grace an Angel's tongue,
Often o'erflow in his melodious fong:
Nor am I fure, nor do I mean to fay,
That ill affections made *his* judgment ftray.

When thofe dread Angels, who appointed are
To cite us mortals to the final bar,
Shall from the clouds, like flaming light'nings,
   fpring,
Auguft, tremendous; fhake the thundering wing;
          And

And blow the solemn trump, whose sound shall spread
The loud alarm, that must awake the Dead;
When *Christ* our Lord, shall issue, glory-crown'd,
With awful pomp of radiant Angels round,
Enrob'd in all the Majesty of GOD,
To judge this World, where once he victim trod,
And shall sit down upon his judgment-throne
Then shall the secrets of all hearts be known.

To a LADY.

WHILE proud *Ambition* meditates a throne,
The papal mitre, or a realm undone,
Dismantled cities, desolated farms,
The pomp, the plunder, and the waste of arms,
To trample Innocence with iron shod,
Intoxicate and drench'd with human blood:
While *Patriot-Britons* seriously dispute
Which wise-head shall be in, and which be out:
While *Avarice* grasps, at one voracious view,
The golden hills of *Indy* and *Peru*;
In fancy bears them to her dark abode,
And groans and staggers underneath the load,
Like fabled Giants, who the mountains hurl'd,
To batter *Jove* from his imperial World:

While

While *Luxury*, in gold and purple dreſt,
On velvet ſofa languiſhes to reſt;
Indulging indolence and ſoft deſires,
Sooth'd with the airs of Eunuchs' wanton lyres,
Till pleaſure's touches and the fuming bowl
Relax the body, ſtupify the ſoul:
While *Sickneſs* toſſes on the wringing bed,
Or on her pillow droops her aching head,
Deſires the light, and yet the light does hate,
Prays now for this, now for another, ſtate,
O'erwhelm'd with anguiſh and convulſ'd with pain,
The furious fever boiling thro' each vein:
While brawny *Toil* each livid limb diſtends,
And plies his engines to laborious ends,
To feed, defend, to pleaſure and adorn
Our feeble race, to pride and miſ'ry born,
Drudging unweary, 'till the ling'ring light
Dies in the weſt, and leaves the world in night:
While ſilent *Study*, lonely and intent
On latent Things, to learn or to invent,
Seems like a ſtatue, motionleſs, to pore
On volumes, as the Miſer on his ore,
Watching for knowledge, 'till the vitals freeze,
Yet nothing gains but folly and diſeaſe:
While thro' the flow'ry meads and verdant woods,
And by the moſſy banks of ſilver floods,
The *genial pow'r of Love* extends her reign,
Tranſporting ev'ry Nymph and ev'ry Swain:

While

While *amorous Sorrow* mourns a lover dead,
Or (still more deep distress!) a lover fled;
With weeping pale, and fix'd her down-cast eyes,
Grief all her thought, her language only sighs,
Sits sweetly mournful, like a smitten flow'r,
A lily drooping in a flooding show'r:
While blooming *Joy*, who, vigorous and gay,
Derides at care, and frolics life away,
Who feasts with Health, and in her charming breast
Sinks to repose (for Health gives all her zest,
Lights up her eyes with ardors, early dips
In rosy dews her love-inviting lips)
I say, while blooming *Joy* parades along
With *Mirth* and *Wit*, with *Music*, *Dance* and *Song*:
While *You*, with finger elegantly free,
Command the needle, pencil or the key,
Or take the air, or some good author find
Richly to store your amiable mind,
Or chearful with your Cousins talk and play,
And spend in gentle ease the smiling day:
I, here serene, find nothing else to do,
But something to amuse myself and You;
Happy, if it may furnish some delight
To You to read, what I for pastime write.

Like Miser's bounty, 'till his death unknown,
While I enjoy it, it is mine alone.
When Fancy's Act is done, the play is o'er;
All vanishes; my pleasure is no more:

Then

Then you may take the scrawl, and read and scan;
And freely make the most of it, You can.

   In this unsettled state, who does not find
The frequent flux and reflux of the mind?
Passions and sentiments now sink, now rise:
A Fool this moment, shall the next be wise.
One cause, at diff'rent times, yields joy and
    sorrow:
To-day's dear follies fade before To-morrow:
We lose our former selves: 'Tis *Wisdom*'s part
To *know the right,* and *there* to *fix* the *heart.*

   Without her guiding beam if *Passion* rove,
With ev'ry object varies hate and love;
Still doubtful where to bend, and where adhere;
As some blind Pilgrim knows not how to steer,
Left in a Wild, directed by the wind,
Which sometimes blows before, sometimes behind.

   Yet half mankind (who but for joy and pain,
Impress'd by twitches, wou'd exist in vain)
By fluctuating follies ever keep
From that perpetual Calm, where they wou'd sleep,
Wou'd eat and drink, and propagate their stock,
Like Oysters crusted on a slimy rock,
Absorbed in a dull and dead repose,
Regardless of all others' joys and woes.

All sense of duty, and all love of truth,
Perhaps extinguish'd in the dawn of youth,
Their giddy follies make them active still,
And useful to the world, tho' meaning ill.
To grasp a clod, and drop it at the grave,
In fields of slaughter to be counted brave,
To gain a place, a title or a string,
To be the fav'rite spaniel of a King,
To gratify mere luxury and pride,
While nothing's meant, nay, all disclaim'd beside,
What glorious deeds, what graces, those impart,
Who are the veriest dæmons at the heart!

    Vice makes Vice useful too in other sort;
(A serious doctrine! now tho' preach'd in Sport)
Useful as natural Evil, to chastise
Its Votaries: Fools scourg'd by fools grow wise.
But O how blest, had Vice been never known!
Then, it is plain, there had been need of none.

    As oft in Nature opposites produce
The same effects, and prove of equal use;
It happens frequently in Morals too,
That Vice effects what Virtue ought to do;
Does Good thro' pride, thro' interest, or thro'
        chance;
Does God and Man in glory more advance.

                              Yet

Yet neither God nor Man needs Vice's aid;
An ugly Monſter, which God never made;
A ſin-born curs'd Deformity, the birth
Of vile abuſe, by godlike Pow'rs brought forth:
It brought diſorder into Nature's plan;
And ſhed a fatal peſtilence o'er man.
Tho' ſometimes Vice the path of Virtue preſs,
Diſguiſed too in Virtue's comely dreſs,
'Tis harlot-art to make her prey more ſure;
'Tis Satan's wile the fooliſh to allure.
If ſometimes Vice does good, ſhe ſtill intends
Evil; in evil to herſelf ſhe ends.
By Vice the world is ever ſunk in woe:
Virtue alone can general bliſs beſtow:
'Tis Virtue only gives, or can poſſeſs,
That all-ſought Prize, *conſummate Happineſs.*

Be your's and mine—O limit not the bliſs!
Let univerſal Nature join in this—
Virtue's pure joy!—In this let all combine;
And all at once be happy and divine!

To a LADY.

I. MADAM, declare—May I, or may I not,
    Presume to write to You, were sermons
        wrote?
Malice wou'd scowl on the address, if shewn:
"*Neighbors, behold the Tempter in a Gown!*"
The Serpent's form, you know, the Tempter bore,
When he beguil'd our Grandam, *Eve,* of yore:
Yet don't suppose him, Ma'am, to shape confin'd
Of limb or coat; he tempts in any kind,
In any dress—so impudent!—'tis known,
He has not blush'd at scarlet or at lawn.
But I to Villains leave insidious views:
I will indulge my folly, to amuse.

I've no pretensions to the Cap of Wit.
"*Good reason why!*"—You mean, it wou'd not fit.
Well! truly humble is my whole design:
I wish to please; but will not toil to shine.

II. Wits are a species of the human Race,
Too often aiming at its last disgrace;
Mere Zanies on the stage of life, in short,
Who rave, to make the dull Spectators sport.

Nay to the best and wisest is decreed
A vain, a poor pre-eminence indeed !
To be but higher hung to public view:
" *The admiration !*"—Aye !—the terror too !
Beheld as Spectres, which, in lonely glades
Gliding by moonshine, frighten rural Maids:
Their use the same; instead of penal law,
To keep the Weak and Wicked under awe.

    Pure Wit the Good and Sensible commend :
But Wit is seldom chosen in a Friend :
For Wit, tho' honor'd, is repuls'd by Pride,
Which never likes a Friend, it cannot guide.
The witty may be virtuous, all admit :
But all imagine danger in a Wit.
So free republics, jealous tho' secure,
Abhor in patriot Kings the Tyrant's pow'r :
So sinners dread, what never yet did ill,
Almighty pow'r, which, as it saves, can kill.

    III. Why Wits are dreaded Reasons may be store;
Some in themselves, and in their neighbors more.

    To those, who deem of honor and of shame
(As wits may do) by vulgar praise and blame,
Error has charms astonishingly strong :
And what, but *this*, tempts erring mortals wrong ?
Justly

Juftly 'tis fear'd, that thofe will greatly err,
Whofe pow'r is great to Vices, men prefer:
But fince the peft by them, it plagues, is nurft,
(I claim your candor) tell me who is worft?
Children thro' life, men gape at Noife and Show;
Count Mifchief brave; and Worth defpife, if flow:
Benevolence, Utility, look mean,
When Pride and glorious Mifchief take the fcene.
Hence Tyrants, Heroes, Orators and Wits,
Who copy Hell in all, that mortals fits:
Hence fchifms, rebellions and contentions fierce
From States to ftalls, throughout the univerfe.
Dreading contempt, all ftart up, to a man,
To be the moft contemptible, they can:
Profeffing honor, all invert its rules:
Affecting wifdom, all at once turn fools:
Madly infringe, that each his claim may prove,
The perfect bond and blifs of nature, *Love.*

God (whofe great end is univerfal peace
And perfect good) commands that crimes may
   ceafe;
Inculcates mercy, mercy moft fublime,
And pardon full, where pardon is no crime;
(That is, where pardon prompts not to offend;
For elfe muft rigor rife, to guard the End)
But who to peace or mercy will incline,

    H   Ev'n

Ev'n tho' commanded by the Voice divine,
When only Mifchief on this Earth can fhine?

" Have you no fpirit, fenfe, nor generous blood?
" 'Tis moſt ridiculous weakneſs to be good."

So preach the Vulgar, fmall and great:—no merit
Is like a choice malignity of fpirit.
The maxim grows, that *Love, to be fincere,*
Muſt twine her tender union faſt with Fear.
Hence firm allegiance Tyrants hope to prove
From fear and admiration, more than love;
They know, fuch grandeur and applaufe belong,
In common vogue, to daring deeds of wrong.

But, generous Spirits! fuch ungenerous rules
Leave to their Authors, Tyrants, flaves and fools!
Nothing can him to guilty wit entice,
Whofe generous foul difdains that fneaking vice,
Love of mean fame, a fond defire to fhare
Applaufe, which Virtue lothes and cannot bear.
The trump of God thro' Heav'n's extent fhall
    tell,
Not who moſt fhin'd, but meant and acted well.
Noble Ambition fcorns a paltry prize:
It foars at views, to which low minds ne'er rife:
It foars at joys and glories grand and true,
Worthy of fouls immortal to purfue.

But

But grant a Perfon of ingenious mind
Upright, and like a guardian Angel kind;
Who both refrains Wit's poignant fhafts to ufe,
And ftrives his neighbor's foibles to excufe;
What does he gain?—What oft fond parents prove
From worthlefs children, infolence for love.
O bafe reward!—If thus men *will* be bafe,
What *can* preferve them from their fate, difgrace?
Many feem with that haughty meannefs born,
Allow them confequence, they pay you fcorn.
Many, thro' luft to fhine, their friends infeft;
And moft affail the brighteft and the beft.
A rancorous envy in the heart does fneak;
Chiefly, among the Worthlefs and the Weak.
Hence, Men of wit muft oft employ the lance,
To teach fuch Fools their infignificance.

Thus Ma'am, you fee, of reafons there be ftore,
In Wits themfelves, and in their Neighbors more,
To make Wits dreaded.——I wou'd not be fo
By any, but a fool and villain Foe.

To a LADY.

WHAT trifling Paſſions little Life annoy?
    Anxieties for bliſs the thing deſtroy.
See Pleaſure This, and Honour That purſues;
This, boundleſs Riches, which he cannot uſe.
Men, pronely bent ill appetites to pleaſe,
To raviſh Pleaſure often murder Eaſe.
The ſon of Honor in this claſs is ſeen,
A ruffian ſpirit, acting all that's mean;
With his own ſpecies evermore at ſtrife,
He makes a baited Badger of his life.
The fool, that ſcrapes to line his dirty neſt,
Robs and is robb'd; ſtill Knave does Knave infeſt:
How happy He, who luckily gets moſt!
Alas! his All is gotten to be loſt!
Alas! alas! can any good betide
Such Compounds baſe of av'rice, luſt and pride!

  Thouſands of ways all-gracious Heav'n applies,
To caution Folly, and bold Guilt chaſtiſe:
All Nature's pow'rs of mechaniſm and will
Exert their force, repreſſing ill with ill:
One fatal moment totally defeats
The fond importance of all vain conceits;
War, deluge, earthquake, a vulcano's rage
Cruſh in a glance the labors of an age:

                      All

All living join to punish or destroy
The life that brings them pestilent annoy.
Yet long experience scarce makes Any find
The real interest of himself and kind,
Charity pure, which best cou'd aid and heal
The various wants and woes, we mortals feel;
And which, when transient objects are no more,
Wou'd make us triumph on the heav'nly shore.

We strive for ev'ry thing, but what we ought;
Forever sure to miss the substance sought,
That *sweet Complacency*, without allay,
The gift of God to them, who God obey;
Sure still to miss th' inestimable prize,
Which in the bosom of *Jehovah* lies,
His *beatific Love*, exhaustless Cause,
Whence Grace on Earth, in Heav'n whence Glory
      flows:
Pious Obedience only can secure
That perfect bliss, eternal to endure.

We take short views, erroneous counsels frame,
Sollicit ruin, glory in our shame;
'Till we, like flow'rs, the beauteous tribes of May,
From hurt or age obnoxious to decay,
Which rifling hand, or careless foot may spoil,
Fade, fall and mingle with our parent soil.
Then, from the ruin in amazement flown,
The trembling Soul shoots into depths unknown,
                            Some

Some blissful Paradise or gulph of woe,
The mansion of the Dead, where spirits go
To wait the grand revival, and the call
To final Judgment; when *Messiah* shall
Award the righteous amaranthine wreaths,
Where pleasures ever flow, and joy forever
    breathes;
Inflict on sinners chains and penal fire,
Where Fiends tormented to torment conspire:
Trial all past, mild Grace no more finds room;
Stern Justice seals the everlasting doom.

 Madam, forgive this moralizing vein,
The solemn theme, the easy humble strain.
I write whate'er emerges into thought:
Perhaps you'd rather, nothing had been wrote.
Since your amusement fondly I intend;
Be pleas'd to pardon, if you can't commend.

 The precious ores of all *Petosi*'s rills
What cassia breathes, odorous myrrh distiles
The fruitage flavor'd by the torrid breeze,
The painted potwork of the vain *Chinese,*
The finest thread of Indian silkworm's toil,
The flax of *Nubia* by the source of *Nile,*
And all with skill inimitably wrought,
That Envy could not grin at finding fault:
In short, to save the trouble of detail,
Shou'd ev'ry point send home a laden sail,

        With

With rich and rare of All beneath the skies,
All, which the Curious and the Courtly prize—
To these a Youth of gallant form and mind,
No soft *Adonis*, nor of Lemnian kind—
If at your feet this Youth and all his store
Presented were—(could Lady covet more?)—
No, not all these preponderate your Desert;
Nor justly poize the virtues of your heart.

This call not flattery, tho' the figure's strong;
Ev'n snarling Critics licence sons of song.
My meaning wishes all, that Earth can give
To make you happy, while on Earth you live:
For tho' in Heav'n above or Earth below
Externals cannot Happiness bestow,
Without that *something*, out of vulgar view,
Divine-born Virtue, which resides with you;
Yet are Externals requisite to Bliss:
God grant you *Those*, as he indulg'd you *This*!

An ODE. To the MUSES.

LIGHTLY touch the quiv'ring strings,
    Airy as the Linnet sings,
Mellow as the pleasing tale,
In silent eve, of Nightingale.
                      O who,

O who, O ye Muses! so gentle and gay,
As blythe as the morning, as blooming as May,
Enliv'ning as sun-shine, refreshing as dew;
O who, O ye Muses! delights us like you?
    You the spark of Love inspire,
    Breathing up the genial fire:
    You point all his golden darts;
    And wing them sharp to tender hearts.
By the stream of a fountain distil'd from the
    rocks,
The margin all thymy, delight of the flocks,
Ye Muses with Sylvans indulgently play:
Go shew me a Monarch so happy as they,
    Study, when she long explores,
    Deep descends or lofty soars,
    Sues ye, as the thirsty slave
    Desires the cooling chrystal wave.
Among mossy cloysters, where Learning and Ease
Combine to bestow all their sweets and degrees
Each Youth importunes you, adoring your shrine,
To carol the orgies of Beauty and Wine.
    Courts, in whose illusive blaze,
    Pleasure's ev'ry phantom plays,
    Your kind solace oft intreat,
    Of Fancy's pangs the healing sweet.
If Envy is wounded by smile or by bow,
The Courtier in coach or in chair flies to you;

                    Unkind

Unkind is bright Beauty, unmil'd awful Pow'r,
Ye mild, ye bright Muses! your comfort's still sure!

On FALSE FRIENDSHIP,

At the Request of a FRIEND.

EAGLES, stooping from above,
   Warn to flight the trembling Dove.
Lions roaring after prey,
Chase the weaker beasts away.
Lo, the honest brutes despise
Perfidy and mean disguise.
Open lies the Spider's snare,
Broke with ease, or shun'd with care.
None allures with friendly smiles;
None with feigned love beguiles:
None of brutal race we find
E'er to ruin wooe their kind.
Like old Satan to deceive,
Man, is thy prerogative!

  Gentle speech, engaging mien,
Hiding enmity within,
Bring the very Fiend to sight,
Garnish'd like a son of light.

Ah,

'Ah, Misfortune never knows
Where to flee, or where repose !
Dangers ev'ry-where surround :
Eager thousands watch to wound.
Few have virtue to be friends;
All pursuing sordid ends.

Some, with childish pride elate,
Friends, but only friends for state;
Fond to have dependence shewn;
Like a Monkey on a throne;
By feign'd kindness bring you low;
By feign'd kindness keep you so.

Some your services to share,
Wondrous kindly speak you fair.
When the Dupe their load has borne,
Meanly then they sneer him scorn :
Oft repay him with a boast,
They, forsooth, oblig'd him most.

Some insidiously pursue
Friendship, with the basest view:
Prompt the open heart to say
What misconstru'd they betray:
Method certain to obtain
Gossip favor, gossip gain.

Fools

Fools, impel'd by childish whim,
Mutable as vapor seem :
Most with Int'rest change their Friends,
Steady but to selfish ends :
Nothing, but a chain of gold,
Their abandon'd hearts can hold.

When we rise, our Luck the while
All congratulate and smile ;
Ever pleas'd, while gratify'd
Their expectance or their pride.
When we fall, the paltry crew
Soon forsake, nor bid adieu.
Soon, if Need follicit aid,
Ev'ry sneaking soul is fled :
Each from conscious guilt will grow
Vilest traitor, fiercest foe ;
Foul detractor will commence ;
Feigning lyes in self-defence :
Crime with crime he will defend :
Works of malice know no end :
Malice in mean Souls will live ;
They who injure ne'er forgive.

Difficulties ever try
Where we safely may rely ;
Point out merits, which we may
Think upon some happy day ;

Point

Point out meaness, which in time
May with blushes own its crime.

Where's the noble soul, that dares
Succor wants and soften cares?
Whom Misfortune well may trust
To restore her from the dust?
Who to aid Misfortune springs
Gladly on Compassion's wings.

Guardian Angels! if ye find
Such a great and god-like Mind,
Let him shine to me confest,
Theme of Song and welcome guest!

IRONICAL ADVICE to a FRIEND.

NO wonder VICE conciliates repute!
    Each Brute associates with his brother Brute,
Who, finely bred, accomplish'd well in Vice,
Would be without it for a Kingdom's price?
It is the mystery, that makes us free,
Like Masons, of the world's Society.
Your Friends will dub you *gratis*, if you please;
Teach you with care, and load you with degrees;
Rejoicing o'er you with sincere delight,
That Hell, thro' them, has gain'd one proselyte:
The host of Angels not rejoicing more,
When cowardly sinners shrink, repent, adore.

Virtue

Virtue unenvy'd thro' this world may pass;
Or furnish wonder, like our Sovereign's Ass: *
But—"Ouns!" cries Bravo—"I abhor to see
"That godly satire on the world and me!
"It checks our freedom, dashes all our mirth;
"And tells such dreams of Heav'n, as sadden Earth.
"Bray!—let it bray in pulpits!—Priests are paid;
"And talking holy nonsense is their trade:
"But 'tis quite shocking to be seen abroad
"In public life!——I hate it like a Toad!"

Virtue no soul of Fashion can endure:
He that is poor, with Virtue *may* be poor.
Would you be rich; rise up a man of mode:
No man of spirit serves or values God:
Religion quit! Religion ever shun!
Religion's Dupes are ruin'd and undone!
Such are for all society unfit,
'Mong men of business or 'mong men of wit.

Go learn the world!——I do not mean, to gaze,
Reflect and moralize; but learn its ways;
Learn and pursue with unrelenting zeal;
And have such sense as others have to feel:
Do not to men as you would have them do;
But do to them as you are done unto.

If

---

* The Queen's Zebra, which at this time drew numbers to see it.

If some choice Spirit robs you in the street;
Make you reprisals on the next you meet.
Right canine fierceness labor to attain:
When any scoundrel bites you, bite again:
Be not outdone; but to the last contest
Great Mischief's glory with the boldest crest.

   Mark this, my Friend!
The World has many ways
For hopeful Youngsters to aspire to praise:
Wealth, honor, pleasure, all, inviting, shine:
Consult thy genius: Which thou lik'st be thine.

  This Globe, my friend, unnumber'd worlds
     contains.
The worlds of pleasures, and the worlds of gains;
The worlds of honor, and the worlds of dress;
The worlds of gaming and of idleness.
The Wise enjoy their own, its farthest hem:
While all beside are Antipodes to them,
Who, as they ween, like Giants in the moon,
Or flies on cielings, walk heels up, heads down.

  Know thy own world: And, lest you act amiss,
Be sure to know no future state to This.
Adapt your knowledge to your present sphere;
For what is wisdom there is folly here.

If you require a comment on my ſtrain,
The Satiriſts will ev'ry world explain.
They ſpend their breath to rail at Vice,'tis true;
But only teach choice Spirits what to do:
And from a jakes drag Vice to public view.
Many had never known, had they not told,
The honorable crimes, at which they ſcold.
Men ſoon embrace what they deride or blame:
Some court ſuch lines, as eaſieſt ways to fame.
Sublime hiſtorians! They with pomp relate
The feats of Vice, her pleaſures and her ſtate,
Firing ambitious youth to emulate:
Each Youth aſpires, with all his pow'rs unfurl'd,
Like *Alexander* to ſubdue a world.

How much it grieves me, gentle Friend! to find
Remorſe and dread of Heav'n unnerve your mind!
So puſillanimous! You ne'er muſt hope
To kill your man, or bravely ſtretch a rope.
Virgins ſhall wed uninjur'd, Gaming fail,
Watchmen walk ſafe, and Wine in caſks grow ſtale,
Luxury ceaſe, the Poor in comfort breathe,
Faction expire, and Worth enjoy a wreath,
Vile Honeſty ſhall proſper—And the Sun,
Before the Conflagration, ſee the world undone!
Nay—Heav'n ſhall triumph, while the ſaints rebel;
And grace and penitence unpeople Hell!

O

O tell it not in Gath!—Sin boldly like the brave,
'Till Satan take your soul, your rotten bones the
    Grave!

A SONG.

THE Muse ne'er diffembles
My Shepherdefs knows;
My Chloe refembles
The fweet blowing rofe.

She fills with good-humour
The light and the air:
Each Seafon is Summer,
If Chloe be there.

The gay and the tender
Thy young bofom move,
With gentle furrender,
To yield unto Love:

'Tis well, O my Charmer!
Thy Shepherd is true;
No rudenefs fhall harm her,
Nor falfhood undo.

'Tis time for the pleasure
Which Love can bestow:
Our moments of leisure,
How swiftly they go!

How late, you remember,
The country look'd gay;
But now comes December;
All joy is away.

Our cot shall be shaken,
Our garlands shall fade;
The Muse be forsaken,
The spring and the shade;

All pleasure shall languish;
Our love last alone;
'Till sickness and anguish—
Alas! We are gone!

To MAIA.

September 10th, 1767.

O Beauteous MAIA! if thy mind
   A due proportion bear,
In worth and pleasing arts refin'd,
No Maiden is more fair.

And who surveys the glittering stars,
With heav'nly splendor shine,
But owns the Ruler of the spheres
In wisdom prov'd divine?

So in thy charming look, serene,
Expression sweetly tells
What mild Divinity within
Thy fair External dwells.

But hold! No adulation stain
The innocent and pure:
'Tis That, which Beauty from the vain
Must, Martyr-like, endure:

What nonsense must affront her ear?
What impudence her eye?
Her fate demands our pity here:
Her triumphs move a sigh.

When Folly pleasingly excels
In artifice of tongue,
Experienc'd Virtue scarce repels
The kind insidious wrong.

May still Discretion safely steer;
May still your fortunes glide,

From

From hidden rocks and quickfands clear,
O'er Life's uncertain tide.

May Heav'n avert tempeftuous ftorms
And from annoyance fpare,
Long, long, the workmanfhip, it forms
With fuch exceeding care.

That ev'ry bleffing may remain,
As ought on earth, unmov'd,
For worth prefer fome happy Swain,
Your chofen, your belov'd.—

For worth—with each advantage more,
Which, added, you can gain;
Let worth be chief; without it, ftore
And titles were but vain.

Mean-while, your pardon foftly fmile
On this intrufive fcrawl;
The firft perhaps in fuch a ftyle,
The laft, that e'er may fall.

This offering, Madam, to your praife
Means only to divert;
Such tribute as a Poet pays
To Beauty and Defert.

To

To the SAME.

The preceding, happening to be sent soon after a little unlucky Incident, which the Author then knew nothing of, it was supposed to insinuate something of Reproof, for which there was indeed no occasion;—The following was therefore intended as an explanation.

MADAM, if happiness were mine to give,
You not one moment should uneasy live:
Rising at will, and flowing to your hand,
Eternal pleasures were at your command;
With perfect health and virtue to enjoy;
(For without virtue pleasures but destroy.)
But all my efforts little can avail:
Things have their course; and mortals must be frail.

O wise Omnipotent! 'tis justly thine
To deal our portions—'tis a task divine,
Suits Thee alone, of whom is understood
What's most expedient for our final good.
I can no more, than wish, advise and aid
With feeble pow'r, my amiable Maid.

Sorry

Sorry I am, my freedom, kindly meant,
Should work so contrary to my intent.
I now repeat it, *at your friend's request*,
To banish doubt, and ease your fluttering breast.
My Billet was, whatever it might seem,
The pure effect of kindness and esteem.
So great a compliment I never pay,
Unless some striking object pass my way.
Few Ladies, Madam, can, or e'er shall boast
Such high encomiums, furnish'd at my cost:
(I prize my compliments!) of those, that do,
Yourself, the last, stand fairest in my view.

I saw, your fallen countenance betray'd
Imbosom'd harm,—which instantly convey'd
A like effect to very conscious me:
For who resists the force of sympathy?
An heart, that could an armed host defy,
Will faint and tremble at a Lady's eye.

But once got wrong, we reel in error still;
And blunt apologies increase the ill:
Excusing and correcting faults before
Will make one fault beget an hundred more:
Perhaps, I'm only adding to my crimes.
Forgiveness, Ma'm! to me and to my rhimes!

Forgiveness

Forgiveneſs grant!—the time may come at laſt,
When we ſhall meet, and laugh at fancies paſt.

When next we meet, reſerve and form be far;
With ev'ry imp of jealouſy and war:
Be our companions ſuch as we may praiſe;
And in whoſe converſe we could ſpend our days;
With ſenſe combining elegance and eaſe;
Ready alike to be pleas'd and to pleaſe:
Above weak arrogance and little guile;
Sincere and chearful as a Cherub's ſmile;
Content and conſtant; knowing both t'employ
Life's fair advantages, and to enjoy;
And, in a word, (where much is underſtood)
Exploring happineſs by being *good*.
Such, might I chooſe, my company ſhould be:
And would not ſuch pleaſe you, as well as me?
Pleaſures in ſuch Society o'erflow!
Pleaſures, which the virtuous only know!

This world ſeems Eden, opening on the ſight
Of joyous youth its treaſures of delight;
Looks all inchanting in life's early ſpring;
Bright Beauty glows; ſoft Love and Pleaſure ſing:
Youth no ſenſation entertains, but joy:
How bland the boſom! and how briſk the eye!
But age advancing, injury invades,
If guilt corrupts not: blooming Eden fades:
Grief

Grief dims the eye with many a briny tear;
Corrodes the bosom unrelenting Care:
Life's changing day with pensive gloom deform
The roaring tempest and the pouring storm:
Fierce heats and frosts efface the finest frame:
Know, thine, O *Maia!* must endure the same.

Such thoughts alone inspir'd me, when I drew
My too bold pen, to write at first to you.
Charm'd with your *Beauty*, anxious to reveal
What, I believe, no duty bids conceal,
I would write something; and, among the rest,
Insinuate advice:—but all in jest!

In jest or earnest, Ma'm, ne'er comes in vain
What your reflexions may convert to gain.
You, prime in youth, conspicuous by your charms,
Require the guard of Caution's strongest arms,
To give protection against Fortune's frown,
Our sex's vice, the envy of your own;
But chiefly, him, who cruelly beguiles,
Concealing ruin under gentle smiles.

Now once again I ardently implore
Your pardon greatly, but your Friendship more;
Then bid farewel.—All happiness ensue!
I humbly kiss your hands.—Dear Miss, adieu!

A

A SONG.

HE.

MY charming *Amanda*, farewel to the snow!
    The yellow-hair'd willow and primroses blow,
Each morning more gay than the former.
Now, copiously breathing in flosculous air,
We'll wander and wanton delightfully, where
Clear swift-running streams gently murmur.

SHE.

See, *Damon*, the birds in the fresh-budding spray,
With frolic and melody joyfully gay,
Transportedly uttering pleasure.
Lo, yonder the solemnly-sweet-cooing dove:
The swallow too merrily twittering love:
Love ravishes all beyond measure.

HE.

More fond than the dove, than the swallow more gay,
Thy *Damon* the raptures of love shall obey.
Our flocks are all wandering whither
The craggy-brow'd precipice wildly adorn

The russet heath tufted and white flow'ring thorn:
Come, dearest *Amanda*, haste thither.

She.

The craggy-brow'd precipice, *Damon*, I fear:
The scene is romantic, but danger is near:
In lonely excursion, so clever,
Some prickle may tear me, or viper asleep
Uncoil from a tuft, or I fall down the steep:
Alas! I were ruin'd forever!

He

No danger, *Amanda*, when *Damon* is nigh,
An holy-like influence beams from your eye,
Whence generous virtue is given.
With life wou'd I guard you in every scene,
Betray! who can perpetrate folly so mean?
Not I, dear *Amanda*, by heaven!

She

With honor attended in *Damon*'s gay form,
I'd wander a desart, unfearful of storm;
And think myself hallow'd from thunder.

He

In love let us join, and thro' life let us go,
Thro' stilness or tempest, thro' sunshine or snow:
No fortune shall part us asunder.

To LOTHARIO.

HOW fares *Lothario?*—Whim will have its way.
They oft talk most, who have the least to say:
The lightliest-loaded is the swiftest beast:
I scribble fastest, when I think the least.
Why, so do all, I ween,   And flippant style
Charms most the Many; makes ev'n Critics smile.
Most people judge alike of men and beer:
" No froth, my boys! No froth! No spirit here!"
If windy froth deliciously o'erflows,
Each wise face, captivated, drops its jaws.
" But what, You cry, means all this vulgar stuff?
Not angry hope!—What all folks mean—a puff.
No company, or good or bad, hard by,
Nor any living Creature, but a Fly!
To read or walk what mortal can endure!
O idleness! how spend this wretched hour?
I'll write to thee, my pleasing Friend—Amen!
There goes the first wild flourish of my pen.

If like Enthusiasts, who their little store
Impart to others, while themselves need more,

Or

Or rather, like vain Prodigals, profuse
Of wealth, ill-given such idoets to its use,
I lavish counsel—well!—Suppose I do,
The folly's mine, the profit's all to you.

My friend, I hear (it founds in ev'ry breeze)
Your heart is much too tender for your ease.
Indeed no wonder, that the amorous Fly
Stings it amain when morn-like *Flora*'s by:
Its gentle texture, if a Nymph instils
One genial charm, in ev'ry fibre thrills:
There sense and beauty cannot fail to please,
And even make the pleasure a disease.
Where'er gay Love unfurls his purple wings,
Each simple Swain his melting folly sings;
Rude Hinds grow tame, the lenient Pow'r adore,
Nor talk obscene, nor jibe and roister more:
If vulgar minds such warm sensations know,
Thine, O *Lothario*! may be thought to glow!

But, O *Lothario*! If thou dreadest care,
Toil, want or anguish, guard thy bosom there.
Tho' beauteous *Flora* claims thy passion well,
And love abounds, yet prudence shou'd excel.
Reasons, which justify thy flame, disswade:
Shall love destroy thy all-accomplish'd Maid?
Can, without Fortune's bounty, Thou and She
From all your worth extract felicity?
                                No!

No!—Mutual Love, which bleſt is bliſs ſupreme,
Wou'd ſwell diſtreſs, and make each pang extreme;
The value high, the ſentiment refin'd
Excite a grief, too mighty for the mind.
Ah, leave to bloom, as you regard her good,
That ſweeteſt Roſe, that ever bluſh'd in bud:
Leave her to bloom ſome wealthier lover's bride:
Be thine the Lily fair amid the ſilver tide.

   Yet, if thine heart, reluctant to ſubmit,
Abhors the thought, purſue expedients fit,
Expedients to ſecure the lovely prize
In full fruition of connubial joys.
My friend! but how? Can either pray'r or force
Incline the Stars to liſten from their courſe?
Deſert is known, and finds reward as ſoon
From thoſe above, as thoſe below the moon.
"*Uſe means! Uſe means!*" is the faſtidious rule
Of ev'ry lucky, ſelf preſuming Fool:
And means avail: But who ſhall chalk the plan?
'Tis chance exalts, occaſion proves the man.
Chance gives occaſion: but, occaſion given,
The uſe—What's more precarious under heaven?
That uſe, which renders one Attempter great,
Will oft another totally defeat.
What nice contingencies, which none foreſee!
How little, Man, thy welfare lies in thee!
                       Beyond

Beyond all sophistry, our pow'r to fall
Is very great; to rise, is very small.

In men's affairs, all just observers know,
There's what no art can stem, an Ebb and Flow.
As curious *Newton* found his glass, by fits,
The sun-beam now reflects and now transmits;
So something secret now repels our force;
Now speeds, beyond our hope, a gliding course.
In short, pursuing learning, fortune, fame,
Great parts and application miss their aim,
Without that due contingency of things,
Whose kind concurrence easy triumph brings.
To mark that moment, if it comes, to guide
Before the gale, and voyage with the tide,
Includes the art of steering to that coast,
Thro' life's main ocean, which we covet most.

Suppose you compass—(and, by all divine!
I wish whate'er is valuable thine!)
An affluent fortune and your lovely fair,
And all that's worthy of a wise man's care;
Enjoyment lies not solely at your will;
There's *Chance* and *Providence*, remember, still.
Oft as a gurge, in hollow mountains pent,
Opens, by steam explosive, sudden vent;
Impetuous, furious, roars it down the steep,
And pours in dreadful journey tow'rd the deep;

Bears

Bears vills and farms, with all their stores of
    grain,
And all the flocks and herds upon the plain;
Sweeps to destruction all, its torrents find;
And leaves broad desolation spread behind:
So something sudden, and beyond our pow'r,
Blasts all our joys.——Then, never be secure!—
Think how the careless at the deluge far'd,
And, like good *Noah*, get an Ark prepar'd.

    'Tis pure Religion, which from woe can save,
Disarm Death's sting, and triumph o'er the Grave.

The Praise of ROME.

From the Greek of Erynna Lesbia.

HAIL! Martial *Rome!* the golden-crown'd!
    High-top'd Olympus Thou hast found,
Which never shall decay;
To thee alone did Fate ordain
The glory of a stedfast reign,
And universal sway.

Thy mighty bonds bind Earth and Sea;
Remotest nations bow to thee;

And Time, o'erturning all,
Still changing scenes, and actors new
For ever leading into view,
Not Time effects thy fall.

Of all, the solar beams adorn,
Thy sons alone are Warriors born,
For conduct and for toil;
In number like the blades, that grow
Where *Ceres* does her bounty sow
Upon a fertile soil.

The VISION.

AN humble *Muse*, unknown to boastful Fame,
No trump requiring to resound her praise,
Regarding not the glories of a Name,
If blest with ease to tune her simple lays,

Wrapt in soft slumbers, late, in Vision saw
Events of years, as Vision may beseem;
Events which did the World's attention draw,
Not undeserving of a Muse's dream.

Lonely reclin'd beneath a broad-spread Oak,
Which old in ages immemorial sprung,
She saw, and at the scene sad silence broke:
Thus started plaintive accents from her tongue.

" O

" O this impious unbleſt age!
" *War*, infernal Fury, prowls;
" Slaughters with enormous rage;
" And, pleas'd with boundleſs carnage, howls.

" O were faculties e'er given
" In cruel deeds to be employ'd?
" Thus to deſtroy and be deſtroy'd?
" Impoſſible! all-ſacred Heaven!

" The Peaſant delves with honeſt toil;
" Upturns the ſurface of his field,
" In pleaſing hope, the furrow'd ſoil
" Will homely neceſſaries yield;

" In hope with labor hard and care
" To feed and clothe his babes and ſpouſe;
" And reſt content and debonair,
" At placid Eve, in ſtraw-built houſe.

" Invain his hope! invain his toil!
" The only fruit deſpair and ſpoil!

" He ſees wild Ravage waſte the field,
" Which late in irkſome ſweat he till'd.
" By trooping ſteeds his harveſt ſpurn'd;
" By cruel hands his cottage burn'd:
" Before his rueful ſtreaming eyes
" His Infants periſh, his Eſpouſed dies!

" But

" But if the Peasant's fate imparts
" No touch to Men's obdurate hearts;
" If, thro' imagination vain,
" They flight the Poor and mock his pain;

" And but to pompous pamper'd Chiefs
" Vouchsafe their sympathetic griefs;
" Behold the Great and their abodes;
" And weep, proud Worms, your mortal
  " Gods!

" The once gay Palace, the once crowded Town
" Stand lonely ruins, monuments of woe;
" Stern *War*, dire issue of *Jehovah*'s frown,
" O'erwhelming, lays them in destruction low.

" The princely Chief, who lately blaz'd
" High in awful grandeur rais'd,
" By multitudes ador'd,
" Deserted dies, biting the clayey sward.

" The peerless She, whose form was dress'd
" In all the brilliance of the East,
" Whose sole disdain'd the ground to tread,
" Roams wild thro' wastes, wishing a
  squalid shedd.

K " See

" See where GERMANIA, with excefs of grief
" Diftracted, mourns her defart lands :
" Difrob'd and mute, defpairing of relief,
" A weeping ftatue like, fhe ftands !

" Her pride of Art, her Nature's ftore,
" Her food and raiment are no more !
" Her forefts fall ; her plains are fpread,
" Lo, here with camps ! lo, there with dead !"

Thus mourn'd the *Mufe*.—Alarm'd, BRITANNIA
   rofe ;
Aided GERMANIA, and reprefs'd her foes.
Whereat the *Mufe* retun'd her grateful lays,
Enraptur'd, to BRITANNIA's praife.

" Glory to great BRITANNIA, who beftows
" On friends protection, clemency on foes !
" Bounteous and merciful, like Heaven !
" *Afk and receive ! Repent and be forgiven !*

" Glorious fhe rofe, in pow'r fupreme,
" Fair Paragon of royal ftate :
" Meek but awful fhone the beam
" Of her bright eyes, whofe look is fate.

" Go

" *Go forth, my free-born Sons!*—she said—
" *Invincible in arms!*
" Forthwith her ensigns broad display'd;
" Day was astonish'd at the shade!
" Her gallant warriors rush'd amain:
" Dreadfully quak'd the sounding plain!
" Air was confounded with alarms!

" Her mighty Navies wing'd the deep,
" And pour'd their thunders as they flew.
" False GALLIA soon was forc'd to weep,
" Her sons no more, her islands few.
" Both *Indies* heard, and trembling saw
" The terrors of BRITANNIA's wrath.
" Barbarians bow'd, and own'd her law
" Most just, tho' terrible as Death.

" Islands and Provinces subdu'd
" She conquer'd only for their good!

" This truth their chearful mien reveals:
" BRITANNIA's gentle sway they bless;
" And curse false GALLIA, while she feels
" What she devis'd for them, Distress.

" Here, curst Ambition, view thy fate!
" O'erthrown, unhelp'd unpity'd lie!
" Nor Man, nor God regrets thy state:
" Ev'n Mercy smiles to see thee die."

But

But whilst the *Muse* thus pour'd along
The transports of triumphant song;
Down from a sable cloud, that shed
Some chilly drops, a Form did glide,
Pallid and sad; it rueful cry'd,
BRITANNIA! GEORGE *is dead!*

Heart-struck and dumb, the pierc'd *Muse* stood,
'Till from her eyes outstream'd a gushing flood,
Which eas'd her panging pain.
Soon as the pow'r of voice she found,
She shriek'd: the Hills affrighted round
Shrunk and shriek'd again.

Soon as regain'd the use of tongue,
She thus in mournful accents sung—

" Immortal be thy glorious fame,
" O GEORGE! as now immense!—Thy name
" Remotest Nations heard with awe,
" Submissive to BRITANNIA's law:
" Thy Name let Times remotest hear
" With wonder; and with praise revere!

" Story, with thee adorn'd, must shine:
" Inspired Bards with emulous design
" Shall paint thy character, great Sire,
" In living colors of ideal fire!

" Each

" Each *Muse*, for love of human race, will shew
" What virtues grac'd thy royal brow ;
" How mad Ambition did thy justice prove,
" The Poor thy providence, the Good thy love,
" And All thy mercy.—BRITAIN, *This* proclaim!
" *This*, all ye *Continents*, who fear'd his Name!
" *This* all ye *Isles*, imbosom'd in the deep,
" Who shar'd his strong protection! Praise and
   " weep!

" 'Tis *yours* to weep! Attune your harps to flow
" Sad songs; and load each sounding note with woe!

   " Whose Word, fate-bearing, like the Voice of
       " God,
" Shall now send *War* invincible abroad,
" To stem th' embattled Vallies, shake the savage
       " Hills,
" And thunder Tyrants from their bloody wheels?
   " GEORGE is no more!
" BRITANNIA weeps upon her naked shore!

   " Ye noble *Council*, *Heroes* brave,
" How will ye mourn around the royal Grave!
     " Ye *Fair*, erewhile like blissful skies
      " Diffusing joy, what aking sighs
" Shall heave your tender bosoms! O what
       " gloom
" Of tearful sorrow darken Beauty's bloom!
                              Anxious

" Anxious *Commerce* shall the Change forego;
" Penurious *Trade* shall mix the general woe:
" As in black state the solemn hearse appears,
" *Toil* shall stand still to shed some filial tears.

" Lament your great Protector dead, ye *Swains!*
" Whose lot was plenty on the peaceful plains,
" While long, beneath his shadowing arm secure,
" Ye sung to Freedom in the festive bow'r.

" Ye lucid Streams, that murmuring glide along,
" Ye Rocks, responsive to the Shepherd's song,
" Resound our woe!—Thou hoary Ocean, mourn
" Thy Monarch dead!—Ye gazing Stars, that
   " burn
" High-thron'd in ether, now, in sign of woe,
" With paler light and pensive influence glow!"

In sobbing verse the *Muse* cou'd grieve no more;
But long, in silence, long did she deplore!
'Till, with a sudden recollection caught,
She thus advanc'd her sorrow-healing thought.

" 'Tis well! 'tis well!—I feel fresh comfort
   " spring!
" Lo, rising fair, I see the *youthful* KING.
" He comes in pow'r and splendor, like the Sun,
" Prepar'd his glorious vernal course to run.

      " On

" On him BRITANNIA bends her flowing eyes;
" As some good Matron, when the Father dies,
" Beholds with fondness her surviving Boy,
" The Father's image, and conceives new joy.
" His chearing aspect gives my breast relief;
" And joy, new joy, has banish'd all my grief!"

While charming admiration siez'd
The *Muse*, and danc'd her bosom pleas'd,
The Yatcht flew o'er to fetch the Bride,
To grace the youthful *Monarch*'s side.
Soon as this Theme of joy appear'd,
The *Muse* exulting thus was heard.——

" British *Muses!* rise prepare
" Lofty strain and dulcet air!
" Our youthful *Monarch*'s destin'd Bride,
" Led by Love, assays the tide;
" Haste to hail the *Royal Fair!*

" Haste, and bring your noble songs,
" Fit to honor British tongues!
" Sacred songs of bold design;
" Songs, that utter flame divine;
" Generous, and becoming Thee,
" *Genius* born of *Liberty*.

Music,

" *Music*, all thy pow'rs employ,
" Breathing pipe and warbling lyre,
" Tun'd to accents, that inspire
" Genial love and festive joy.

" *Britons*, of your loyal choice,
" On the patriot-scene attend !
" Delighted Angels list'ning bend,
" And aid the chorus with their voice.

" Hark ! how swell the rapturous lays !
" Lofty sense and melting sound !
" Lo, the charmed dolphin plays ;
" Tam'd sea-monsters gambol round.

" *Ocean* owns his sovereign Bride ;
" Still'd is ev'ry boisterous roar :
" Gently heaves the rolling tide,
" And calmly murmurs on the shore.

" *Heav'n*, well-pleas'd to see Her come,
" Serenely sheds a brightening smile ;
" And bids the softest-winged gales
" Gently spread the bosom of the sails
" To speed dear CHARLOTTE home,
" A grace peculiar to this favor'd *Isle*.

                              " Nuptial

" Nuptial *Guardians*, bind their loves
" Fond and firm as Turtle-doves :
" In your wreath all bleffings twine,
" Virtuous pleafures, joys divine.
" *Friendſhip, Friendſhip* ftill be there,
" Zeft of pleafure, balm of care.

" O bleft *Friendſhip*, eldeft-born
" Thou of *Virtue*, Fair divine!
" The blown mofs-rofe and bloffom'd thorn
" Breathe no fweetnefs, match'd with thine!

" When wintry forrows nip our mortal bloom,
" She melts them as the fun; or gilds their gloom,
" As the moon's orb, with filver beauty bright,
" Sheds chearfulnefs thro' the cold vault of night.

" GEORGE and CHARLOTTE on the throne,
" May *Glory* radiate the crown;
" The heav'n-born fifters *Peace* and *Love*
" Defcend triumphant from above;
" Meek-ey'd *Virtue* rear her brow,
" Scoffing *Vice* be humbled low,
" While *Equity* with fteady hand
" Lifts her balance o'er the land.

" Join, *Mufes*! let your voices fill
" The Court, the City and the Vill!

Let

" Let humble Cot and stately Dome
" Welcome royal CHARLOTTE home!

" Let joy alone be heard and seen,
" While you exalt the raptur'd strain.
" Huzza! Long live the KING and QUEEN!
" Long and happy! Long and happy!
" Long live and happy reign!"

BRITANNIA lovely smil'd, and glow'd
    In extasy of pleasure:
Honors and *Victories* thronging bow'd;
And pour'd into her lap their treasure.

Meanwhile HISPANIA's sullen pride
BRITANNIA's glory can't abide.
In murmurs first She did revile:
" *I scorn*, She cry'd, *that saucy Isle!*"
At length, out-flew her shining sword;
A lightening glance it sent.
HISPANIA, rue that scornful word!
That action rash repent!

BRITANNIA, cool and und smay'd,
Collected, the mad act survey'd.
To arms, she cries, *my free born sons!*
To arms they fly.—Her dying Dons
HISPANIA soon complains;

                        Her

Her lov'd Havannah is no more!
Her warriors gasp along the shore,
Or drag inglorious chains.

Her silver-freighted *Galeots* yield
Their cargos on the wat'ry field
T' enrich the British *Tars,*
Whose hearts rejoice to meet the foe,
Whose hands strike home the conquering blow,
And make a sport of wars.

Humbled in heart, Britannia's foes
Conciliating terms propose.
Then *She,* dread Empress of the main,
With *Victory* combin'd,
Bound on the jaws of *War* a chain,
Still pleas'd to spare mankind.

Peace, fled to Heav'n, she did recal,
To heal the groaning Lands.
No longer War shall vex the Ball!
Britannia so commands.

Lo, poiz'd on light embroider'd wings,
Peace hovers, ready to descend;
Her Cornucopy flowing brings,
A grateful present to her friend.

Britannia

BRITANNIA, pleas'd, the boon admires;
And to her wife and generous breaft,
Which *Virtue*'s ardent flame infpires,
Embraces glad the heavenly Gueft.

What joy foft-hearted Virgins prove,
Infpir'd with *Mufic* and with *Love*;
Or Babes in the indulgent fmile
Of Her, who rears them with a tender toil;
Such feels Britannia in fair *Peace*'s arms,
Returning after *War's* alarms.

As genial dews the air diftils,
So *Peace* with glad'ning vigor fills.
Peace, fweet as groves when bloffoms rife,
Calm as a fountain, mild as fummer fkies,
Her bleffings round as dews diftils,
And ALL with glad'ning vigor fills!
So vernal funs the winter's clouds remove;
And all is light fecundity and love.

 The feftive board was richly crown'd;
 Huzzas and bumpers circled round.
 To *Liberty* was crown'd the Oak:
 The Cannons roar'd—The *Mufe* awoke.
       DAVID'S

POEMS

DAVID's LAMENTATION for SAUL and JONATHAN.

THY Glory, *Israel*, is slain!
 How are the Mighty fallen! dead on
  thy rocky plain!
 O tell it not in *Gath*! nor known
 Let it be made in *Askelon*!
 Virgin Philistines will joy!
 Virgin Heathens triumph high!

Mountains of Gilboa! no dew,
Distilling mild, descend on You!
 Nor show'r nor offering bless your soil!
There, *there*, our great dishonor lay!
The shield was vilely cast away!
There fell the armor of the brave!
The shield of *Saul*, as of a slave,
 Anointed He with holy Oil!

 From the mighty Chiefs, that bled,
From the blood of numbers slain,
The bow of *Jonathan* ne'er fled;
Nor turn'd the sword of *Saul* invain.

 The royal Sire, the royal Son,
In life were *Israel*'s joy and pride;
(As Eagles swift, as Lions strong)
And in their death did not divide.

Weep,

> Weep, gentle hebrew Virgins, weep!
> Your Monarch lies in everlasting sleep!
> He deck'd your beauteous forms in gold;
> And made you lovely to behold.
>
> How are the Mighty fallen amid the war!
> Thou, Prince, upon thy lofty rocks wast slain!
> To me, my brother, wast thou very dear!
> For thee, my brother, swells my heart with pain!
> Thy love to me was vast! above
> The fondest tender Virgin's love.
>
> How are the Mighty fallen! how set our Glory's
> star!
> O how have perish'd all the weapons of the war!

ODE 15. Of Book II. of HORACE, 1751.

GRAND Fabrics rise so thick upon the plain,
Few fields for tillage interspers'd remain.
Immense Canals, extending on each side,
Draw curious strangers to admire our pride.
Unmarry'd planes their shady boughs entwine,
Where elms before sustain'd the loaden vine.
Violets and myrtles, and a world of those,
Which only gratify a dainty Nose,

A

A barren odor to the breeze afford,
Where teeming olives paid the former Lord.
Umbrageous laurels in long ranges run,
To screen the drunkard from the mid-day sun.
All these our Fathers neither saw nor heard:
Not rigid *Cato*, with his ell-long beard;
Nor mighty *Romulus*.—The private state
Of each was small, and the republic great.
No private Portico was seen to rear
A front superb against the polar Star.
The laws let none an humble cot despise;
But bade munitions, strong and costly, rise;
And stately Temples, polished and hewn
By ablest artists, out of finest stone.

ODE I. Of PINDAR's OLYMPICS.

WATER is the first of Things:
    Gold, with rich resplendence bright,
Shines in wealth, as fire that flings
Radiance thro' the vault of night.
High atchievements would'st thou praise,
My genial Spirit!—hast thou spy'd
A star out-shine the solar blaze,
Gilding the etherial void?
Nothing can we found to Fame,
Nobler than Olympic Game.

                         Thence

Thence to lofty lyric song
Attunes each learned Bard melodiously his tongue;
To mighty Jove each lyre is ftrung,
When grand proceffions bend their feet
To *Hiero*'s rich and happy Seat.

Hiero, holding glorious reign,
Sicilia, o'er thy fleecy plain,
Every fweet of Virtue fips,
And Mufic's flow'ry beauty taftes,
As we enjoy with curious lips
Exhilerating feafts.

Take and ftring the Dorian lyre,
If *Pifa*'s, *Pherenicus*' Glory
Lofty pleafing airs infpire,
Since by *Alpheus*, fam'd in ftory,
The fiery fteed
His Lord, the Syracufan King,
A Lover of the Racer's ring,
To Victory thunder'd with prodigious fpeed.

His Glory fhines
Upon the peopled fhore
Of *Pelops*, whom the mighty pow'r,
Neptune, who the lands confines,
Dearly lov'd, when *Clotho* drew
His vital Thread, reftor'd anew:

His

His ivory-shoulder'd arm,
Graceful, cast a matchless charm.

Many are those marvellous tales,
To superstitious audience sweet:
Fable more than Truth prevails,
So charming is the painted Cheat.

Fancy, drawing heav'nly forms,
Alluring, flattering unto view,
Magic wonders oft performs,
Dissembling very Falshood true:
But future ages are the test:
Mature Experience teaches best.

Of ruling Gods let mortal tongue
Speak decently sublime;
Are then our dark Ideas wrong,
More venial is the Crime.

Son of *Tantalus!* my lays
Shall thee beyond thy Fathers praise.

Immortal Gods, invited, come
To feast at splendid *Sypulum*,
When there thy Father once repaid
The Banquet, they before for him had made.

The God, who bears the forked mace,
Prudence yielding to desire,
Snatch'd thee in his golden chaise
High to the dome of Heav'n's all-ruling Sire.—

   Such fate did *Ganymedes* prove,
In after-times, belov'd of *Jove*.—

When thou no more wast found,
Nor to thy sorrowing Mother brought
By those, who long had vainly sought;
Slander's assassin tongue, that kills with secret wound,
Pronounc'd thee boil'd, dissected, eat,
And mangled in a strange inhuman treat.

   I blush that Folly should conceive
So grosly of the sky.
Gluttons the Gods!—could Ignorance believe?
Loss is the wages of a lye.

   True, if the Gods did ever condescend
To be a mortal's Guest and Friend,
Tantulus was He:
But long he could not bear
His over disproportion'd share
Of too refin'd felicity.

  Pain on satiety attends.
Above his aking head
Jove a ponderous stone suspends,
His constant toil and endless dread.
In wretched indigence he breathes,
Consum'd with fruitless toils;
Because he robb'd the hallow'd Cups
Of immortality, where sups
The holy Synod, crown'd with gorgeous wreaths;
And also made his Guests profane the sacred
    spoils.

  Whoever thinks his morals hid
From sight Divine, mistakes indeed!
  Hereon the Gods, in ample grace,
His Son restored to the mortal race.

  He, in vivid bloom of life,
His chin with early velvet drest,
Amorous fancies in his breast,
Fair *Hippodamia* sought to wife.

  Lone-wandering by the foamy flood,
In gloomy night, the Lover cry'd,
" O *Neptune!* Monarch of the tide!"
Forthwith the God presenting stood.
To whom the Youth—" O God of Seas!
" If ought the joys of *Venus* please,

       " Defraud

" Defraud *Oenomaus*'s spear!
" Make me the happy Charioteer!
" Grant me Victory! For know,
" After thirteeen Lovers slain,
" Bright *Hippodamia*, goddess of their vow,
" A Virgin, Virgin, does remain.
" True, arduous trials suit not feeble man;
" But since we all must die,
" Why wish to lengthen out my span
" With indigence and infamy?
" Be mine the grand exploit!—O bless
" My gallant essay with success!"

He spoke; nor dy'd his words in air:
The God, propitious to his pray'r,
Presents a golden chariot, join'd
To steeds impetuous as the wind.

Oenomaus, thence overthrown,
His honor and his Virgin lost.
She bore six Champions, Heroes of renown,
Valor evermore their boast.

Now *Pelops* numbers with the mighty Dead;
His tomb, *Alpheus*, on thy margin stands;
Close by that Altar his Remains are laid,
Revered most of foreign lands.

Olympic

Olympic sports their fame around
In that of *Pelops* wide display,
Where matchless speed and strength are crown'd
With glory sacred from decay:
The Victor spends his future days
In honor, calm content and ease;
With still this blessing to befal,
The final moment, which arrives to all.

To me, by rule of Chivalry, belongs
To crown the Victor with Eolic songs:
For who, among the modern race,
Tho' Wit and Grandeur both combine,
Shall, with inimitable grace,
The lyric Garland twine?

Heav'n prosper my designs!—O King!
If Heav'n prolong Thee aid,
To thy swift wheels my Muse shall sing
Far sweeter strain
Upon the sunny Cronian plain,
Where grows no sylvan shade.

For *this* the Muse for me, with care,
Does ev'ry choicest shaft prepare.

Let others shine in other things:
Supremacy belongs to Kings.

Indulge

Indulge no more Ambition's eye;
Be it thine
Upon a royal Throne to shine:
Be it mine
Thy royal presence to enjoy;
And be thro' native Greece renown'd,
As with the palm of wisdom crown'd.

ODE II.

Of PINDAR's OLYMPICS.

YE harp-inspiring HYMNS! what God or King,
What Hero shall I choose to sing?
Pisa sprung from awful *Jove*,
Emperor o'er the Thrones above.
Hercules condignly claims
The institution of Olympic games,
Oblations of his martial spoils
After long victorious toils.

But tune my lyre to *Theron* glorious,
In the Chariot-race victorious;
Kindly, hospitably great!
Pillar of the *Agrigentine* state!
His Country's tutelary Pow'r,
Of noble Ancestry the flow'r,

Who,

Who, long with laboring counfels fill'd
To make their Country fafe and free,
The facred feat of Rivers held,
And were the eye of *Sicily*.
Thence days of liberty and pleafure,
Crown'd with honor, deck'd with treafure,
Days, which wealth and glory gave,
Rewarding Virtue in the Brave.

O fon of *Rhea!* Thou fupreme
O'er high *Olympus*, o'er the Game!
Song-admirer! I implore
Thy bounty to their native fhore,
And progeny forevermore.

Not Time, the hoary fire of all
Emerging iffues, can recal
What once is paft, or right or wrong:
Oblivion with fuccefs may rife;
For Mifery dies,
Subdu'd among
A profperous hoft of Joys,
When GOD commiffions from above
Sublime Auxiliars, wing'd with love.

Inftance, now in bleft abode,
The Maids of *Cadmus*, long opprefs'd:
For gloomy Evil quits each breaft,
Overcome of ftronger Good.

See *Semele*, who panting fell
With tresses flowing, at the wound,
Infix'd in flaming thunder's found—
See *Semele* in glory dwell,
Rejoicing in the joyful love
Of mighty *Pallas, Bacchus, Jove.*
Ino too, where *Nereus* reigns,
As Rumor tells the tale, obtains
Among the daughters of the sea
A blessed immortality.

The date of life is not decreed;
Nor do we know when tranquil Day,
The son of Morn, will grant us way
From earth; and lasting joys succeed.

Pains and pleasures, rolling tide,
Assail mankind on ev'ry side.

Fortune, ruling o'er the birth
Of Joys, from Deity that flow,
Brings too Calamities on earth,
Perversely blending both below.

Hence *Oedipus* his Father slew;
And prov'd the oracle too true.

Erynnis

Erynnis saw the guilty deed:
And, vengeful, flew his martial feed.

   The haplefs *Polynices* flain,
Therfander only did remain,
Who, great in fports and the embattled plain,
With firm alliance aided thofe
Noble fires, whence *Theron*'s life-blood flows.

   Ænifidemus' Son! to Thee belong
Heroic verfe and lyric fong!
Him olympic glory crown'd:
His Brother's name
Pytho refounded, the *Ifthmus* did refound,
Who, emulous of hallow'd fame,
Twelve-times in race the flowery crown,
Bore away with high renown.

   Whoe'er the flowery crown fhall bear,
Thenceforth is free from anxious care.

   When with Virtue Riches join,
Both improv'd in luftre fhine,
Both, lending mutual aid,
Support and guide the toils of Care,
Our pilot, our effulgent ftar,
Conducting man thro' Nature's fhade.

The Virtuous know a future state;
What miseries behind
Pursue the guilty mind,
What woes on dying sinners wait.

Whatever crimes are done
In *Jove's* wide Empire underneath the sun
Are punish'd with severe decree,
The sentence of Necessity.

Serenest nights, serenest days
The righteous evermore enjoy;
No fearful danger e'er dismays,
No grievous tasks annoy:
They neither plow, they neither sail,
Nor dread to see their plenty fail.
With endless bliss among the Gods
In glory are the just enrol'd;
While sinners groan in dire abodes,
Tremendous to behold!
Whoe'er with vigilance control
The devious motions of the soul,
To *Saturn's* happy seat remove,
Along the starry path of *Jove*.
There ever blows the freshest breeze
Upon that blessed Isle,
Where pleasant odors golden flowers exhale,
Springing in that purer soil,

Or waving on the shady trees,
Or in the silver streams, that glide along the vale,
Rings and Coronets denote their state,
Ensigns righteously bestow'd
By *Rhadamanthus*, great Judge-advocate
Of Father *Saturn*, *Rhea*'s Lord,
Throughout the universe ador'd,
Awful sovereign GOD.

   In that nobility divine
Cadmus and *Peleus* right honorable shine:
And *Jove*, subdu'd by *Thetis*' pray'r,
Achilles too translated there,
By whom great *Hector*, *Troy*'s firm Tower,
Troy's armed Rampire, overthrown,
In dust inglorious lay;
Cycnus bow'd down to Death's dread pow'r;
And *Æthiops*, offspring of the *Dawn*,
Forgot his parent's genial ray.

   My Quiver yet has darts in store,
A volley wing'd to sound in Wisdom's ear;
But Folly understands no more
Without a dull Interpreter.

   Those alone I call the Wise,
Who, born on wings of native Genius, rise.

                                 Learned

Learned Plodders, far below,
At Genius, high above,
Clamor inceſſant, like an envious Crow
Againſt the ſoaring bird of *Jove.*

Bend the bow, and point the dart!
My Soul! where muſt the arrow fly,
Tip'd with benevolence of heart,
And wing'd with glory ne'er to die?
To *Agrigentum!* go!
Ye gods atteſt, for gods ye know,
No City thro' the Grecian land
Theſe hundred years ſhall find
A hand more firm, a heart more kind,
Than *Theron*'s heart and hand.

But Envy longs to ſcale his fame;
Injurious with her noiſy throng,
Beſieging cloſe with hand and tongue,
Would ſtrike the glorious ſtandard of his name.

Go count the ſand upon the ſhore,
Yet thy Arithmetic will fail
Theron's noble deeds to tell:
His large benevolence is more
Than countleſs ſand upon the ſhore.

ODE

ODE III.

Of PINDAR's OLYMPICS.

INDULGENT Pow'rs! attention deign!
Tyndaridæ and *Helen* fair,
Lady of the beauteous hair!
Renowned *Agragas* shall boast my strain,
A flow'r of elegance and skill
For *Theron*'s steeds invincible.

The Muse attends, while I compose
New lays of *Dorian* epic sound:
With majesty the music flows;
Admiring Silence listens round.
The Garlands in their manes entwin'd,
Of me this arduous boon require;
The mellow pipe and song combin'd,
The sweetly-warbling lyre,
Joining concert with my lays
To noble *Theron*'s noble praise:

Pisa requires, to whom belongs
Prerogative to claim;
Whose Chiefs divinely utter'd songs
Immortalize in glorious fame:

Ev'n

Ev'n thofe, to whom, as *Hercules* bequeath'd,
The lawful Arbiter allows,
On their diftinguifh'd foreheads wreath'd,
The glory of the Victor's brows,
Green Olive—

Which He victorious brought
From *Ifter*'s fhady fpring;
The *Hyperboreans* firft befought,
Adorers of the folar King.

Revolving glory in his mind,
Jove's royal foreft fearching round,
At length the fpreading plant he found,
A common bleffing to mankind,
Beft becoming Virtue crown'd.

Then Altars to his Father rofe,
When did the Moon her globe unfold
Full on the dappled evening's clofe,
Pompous in her chair of gold.

Then He olympic fports conceiv'd,
Whence Olympian Æra came,
Upon the rocky banks atchiev'd
Of much renown'd *Alphean* ftream.

But

But in the parched *Cronian* vales
No foreſt ſpread
The green, the cool, the pleaſant ſhade;
'Twas deſart, blown with ſultry gales,
Open to the glowing blaze
Of all the Sun's inclement rays.

Then thought he to remove to where,
Returning from *Arcadia*'s mountains,
Diana's hoſpitable care
Reliev'd him at her ſilver fountains,
A pleaſant land, which *Iſter* laves,
Of winding vales and hollow caves.

Neceſſity, ſeverely kind,
Had then his toils adorn'd,
When *Euryſtheus* had enjoin'd
To fetch the celebrated Hind,
Golden-horn'd—
Which He, devoting to the ſhrine
Of chaſte *Diana*, made divine—

Diana, ſhewing him this land, where cold
Congealing Boreas never blows:
There ſtood he wondering to behold
The ſtately arbors; there he choſe,
Smit with the pleaſures of the ſcene,
To mark the future courſe,

Winding

Winding twelve-times the hills between,
For nimble charioteer and flying horse.

 His presence dignifies the feast,
With *Læda's* sons divine,
Umpires, when he explores *Olympus'* hill,
Who mark the combatants, that shine
In vigorous feats, or study best
To guide the flying wheel.

 Hence, O my soul! the prize of fame
Unto the *Emminidæ* came!
To *Theron* hence did glory flow,
Which the *Tyndaridæ* bestow;
'Cause they devoutly 'mong the rest
Do solemnize the sacred feast.

 Is water the first element—or gold
The brightest gem in riches seems?
Then *Theron's* virtues are extol'd
To *Hercules'* pillars, glory's wide extremes.

 Beyond whatever lies,
Whatever's hid in store,
Impervious is to fool and wise;
Nor shall my folly grasp at more.

ODE

ODE IV.

Of PINDAR's OLYMPICS.

Glorious God of rolling Thunder!
   Awful *Jove!*
Ruling *Ætna, Typhon* under;
Hundred-headed Giant strong,
Groaning loudly, groaning long,
Loads of flaming rocks above!
Me thy circling hours sent forth
With various mellow lyre,
To celebrate superior worth
In all, who gallantly aspire.

  Succeed our friends in noble views,
How sweetly cordial are the news!

  Son of *Saturn!* kindly deign
Acceptance of my choral strain;
Of virtue bright
The fairest most enduring light.

  See *Psaumis* come!
Pisæan olive round his hair.
See him hasten joyful home,
To reap a crop of glory there!

  His rising wishes Heav'n fulfil!
For I his future worth foretel;
His generous care of gallant steeds;
His chief delight in liberal deeds;

His ardent love of human kind:
Rich harveſt of a noble mind!

O let not fiction ſtain my mouth!
Fact is the honeſt teſt of truth.

Thence, *Clymenus*, thy ſon aſhames
The perfidy of Lemnian dames:

When, clad in brazen mail, he won,
Advancing to *Hypſipyle*,
Briſkly he ſeiz'd the victor's crown,
Exclaiming—" *I am He!*"

Ready both in heart and hand!
Fit for action and command!

Thus oft with glad ſurpriſe we find
The hoary head in youth appears;
A prudent and capacious mind,
Beyond the promiſing of years.

On Pestilence *among the* Turks, *and* War
between them and the Russians, 1771.

" UNPRISON *Peſtilence* and *War!*"
  The Voice almighty wrathful ſaid:
Forthwith the dark Abyſs expanded wide its jaws;
         Abhorred

Abhorred *Pestilence* arose:
Her foggy wings infect the air;
Her baleful eyes shoot keen despair;
And scorpions issue from her hideous head.

Where'er she bends her noisom flight,
Loud *Lamentation* howls behind;
Dolorous *Care* consumes the night;
Each day presents so dire a sight,
Beholders wish extinct the light,
Or that their visual orbs were blind.

War, cas'd in mail of solid fire,
Seem'd some portentous Comet's blaze:
" Yoke to my brazen car, he cries,
" The Hyperborean Eagle black.
'Tis done:—Swift as the wind he flies:
His course the sons of Earth and Heav'n admire:
On *Guilt* his vengeful thunders graze;
Delusion shrieketh at the crack.

Where *Tyranny* and *Lust* of late,
Impiously consecrated, reign'd;
And, rudely arrogant in mighty state,
Oppress'd mankind, and God profan'd;
There, in their gorgeous domes, *Dismay*
Blasts all their pride, spoils all their play:
Tyranny

Tyranny raves with rage and fear;
While pallid *Lust* lies swooning near.

" Shall *Servitude* her goading Irons knap?
" Shall *Innocence* go free?
" Shall *Chastity* her virgin lap
" Pure preserve, O *Lust*! from Thee?

" Poignant curses!"—mad *Delusion* cry'd,
And flung her spangled turbant on the ground:
Her sabre fell, and naked left her side:
Her crescent turn'd to blood:
Appal'd the *Pow'rs of Darkness* stood;
And *Hell*, more gloomy, groan'd all round!

Occasion'd by reading Miss CARTER'S POEMS, 1765.

FAIR celestial, found below!
   Willing I this tribute give:
What Devotion doth bestow
Goodness kindly will receive.

Tuneful birds, in vernal eves,
Sweetly heavy moist and mild,
'Mong the forest's velvet leaves,
Mellow sing their love-notes wild.

O'er great Nature's feast of joy,
Odors breathing from each tree,
They delightful notes employ,
Yet they fail to charm like Thee.

   Sappho ev'ry fading flow'r
Rifled in the Cyprian groves,
Venus her adored Pow'r,
Drawn in am'rous pomp with Doves:

   O unlike her Hymns and thine!
O unequal in their force!
Thine to make the soul divine
Strong as hers to make it worse!

   Numbers gay *Anacreon* stole
From the beam-encircled Pow'r,
Soft and easy as his Soul;
Thine *Eliza!* please me more.

   Young may nurse in nightly cells
Holy rage; or *Gay* impart,
Mildly in his simple tales,
Morals worthy of his heart:

   Thompson his description join;
Or in airy Visions rise
Collins, fancifully fine:
Carter shall not want a prize.

                         Noble

Noble *Shakespear*, sacred Name!
Britons ever shall adore;
First in Merit as in Fame;
Equal to behold no more:

Pindar, fierce, in light'ning drest,
Grand Enthusiast! raves with skill;
Glowing like his Heroe's breast,
Rapid as his flying wheel:

Homer, bold in epic Song,
Virgil, cool and curious, sings;
Milton, with angelic tongue,
Personates the KING of Kings:

Dryden's fire my soul does touch;
Pope's fine art, politely free ⸺
Glorious Poets!—O but such
Soft enchantment dwells with Thee!

Pious *Carter*! happy merit!
Fam'd *Anacreon*'s sweetness flows
Thro' thy numbers, while thy spirit
Ardently seraphic glows.

Angels, glory-crown'd above,
Charming Songster! heav'nly Fair!
Wise! divinely wise! will love
Thee, sweet Partner in their care.

Thee on bleſt triumphant wings
Bear, who'ſt early underſtood
Well to praiſe the KING of Kings;
Endleſs office of the Good!

To the Reverend Mr. ATKINSON, *with* ALLAN
RAMSAY's POEMS (*which he had lent the
Author*) *returned,* 1772.

DEAR *Atkinſon!* the Sangs of *Allan*
Prove him a ſnell and canty Callan.
He ſtow'd of wit, at leaſt a gallon
                    In his brain-pan;
And eke of vanity, to pal ane,
                    A ſcottiſh Can.

His verſes ſcurl wi' mickle eaſe,
Saft and ſonorous, flee to pleaſe:
A ſweeter Chiel ane ſeldom ſees
                    'mang Poets rareſt,
Does he the Braveſt tent to bleeze,
                    or eke the Faireſt.

Aften he hits (not ay, 'tis true)
The laſt-won charm, the rythmus due.
Wow, Man! but then his pickland whieu
                    Is ſaul-inchanting;
A wee mair Thought to mind his Cue
                    Is a' that's wanting.
                        Majſtly

Maistly he tals the wale of sense,
With gracefu' native negligence:
He only borders on offence
     Thro' vain neglect:
Some lines rin law and feebler hence,
     They're incorrect.

But in a Paradise, where shine
Beauties luxuriantly divine,
On whate'er side you cast your eyn,
     It were no weel,
As if thro' envy to repine,
     Like the auld Deel.

Thank thee, kind *Atkinson!* but mair,
Thank gentle *Ramsay* for my skair
Of sic refin'd ambrosian fare,
     And sic nice glee:
The like, I trow, is unco' rare,
     Ee'n God be wi' y'.

An

Scotch Words explained.] *Sangs*, songs. *Snell*, firm and acute. *Canty*, jovial. *Callan*, a boy, a wag. *Pal*, Pall. *ane*, one. *Scurl*, slide. *wi'*, with. *mickle*, much. *Saft*, Soft. *Slee*, sly, artful. *Chiel*, a free expression for Person. *Saldom*, seldom. *'Mang*, among. *Tent*, mind, attempt. *bleeze*, praise. *aften*, often. *Wow*, an interjection of Joy. *Whieu*, whistle. *Saul*, Soul. *Wee*, little. *Mair*, more. *a'*, all. *maistly*, mostly. *tals*, tells. *Wale*, choice, best. *gracefu'*, graceful. *rin*, run. *law*, low. *Eyn*, Eyes. *no*, not. *weel*, well. *auld*, old. *Deel*, Devil. *skair*, share. *sic*, such. *unco'*, strangely. *wi' y'*, is *with ye*, pronounced as one long syllable—*Wee*.

An ODE.

BEFORE the Sleepers in the brake,
Before the morning eye-lids wake,
In rapture wake my grateful lays!
To *Him*, for whom my Lyre is ſtrung.
Each glowing boſom, tuneful tongue
In concert join with holy praiſe!

To *Him* ſupreme, who reigns alone,
Almighty King, eternal Throne!
Ten million Worlds, ten million Suns,
Beneath his footſtool rolling ſhine,
Directed by his eye divine:
Where he commands the Comet runs.

Archangels, rob'd in plumy gold,
Whom wings of living flame infold,
Who guide the globes and poize the ſpheres,
Adoring to his footſtool bend,
And, light'ning, haſten, if he ſend
His greeting to this vale of tears.

He bids them guard a good Man's way;
His bidding the bleſt Hosts obey:

All nature speeding at his call,
Ev'n Fires grow mild and Tempests cease;
The Saint finds safety, health and peace,
Where battles rage and thousands fall.

If wicked Fiends, perverse as free,
If Men, who mock his dread decree,
Devise our bane by force or guile;
He frowns the guilty Vile away,
Sore agonizing with dismay;
The Just reviving at his smile.

O Ruler of eternal Skies!
O Ruler holy, good and wise!
Indulgent Sire, with mercy's rod!
Our suppliant Souls we pour to thee,
Our last appeal in ev'ry plea,
Our Evidence, our Judge, our God!

Unequal to the glorious Theme,
My Sonnet creeps like feeble stream,
That down the mountain weeps, and wails
Among the pebbles, as it flows,
Until it sink in dead repose,
Absorbed in the spacious vales.

To a CLERGYMAN, who complain'd of his PEOPLE.

THO' (as your lines complain) your audience scorn
The Preacher's council and his Master's call,
Think not their case so utterly forlorn,
That they deserve no past'ral care at all.

But as the Sun expends his golden rays
On objects of all kinds, from pole to pole;
So Thou, to Good and Bad, let wisdom blaze;
Diffuse the fair ideas o'er each soul.

Truth, pow'rful Truth, will ev'ry bosom pierce;
And, like its Patron, who redeem'd mankind,
Will melt the obstinate, controul the fierce,
Alarm the deaf, illuminate the blind.

" What!" you exclaim, " shall I with feeble
    " voice
" Labor divine perswasion to apply
" To Him, who only dozes at the noise;
" And, downy-wrapt on earth, disdains the sky?"

Ah! let him doze!—Awake, he might esteem
Thy feeble voice, divine perswasion, cheap:
So lull'd, he hears an Angel in his dream;
And learns the song of *Moses* in his sleep.

Much

Much is he charm'd, tho' heedless he appears;
As is the careless Swain, who, on his hill
Drooping to slumber, unattentive hears
The liquid wailings of the passing rill.

He wakes refresh'd, as from divine repose,
Thinks still he hears, and listens for the note;
Recals the Sense, acknowledges the cause,
And blesses the Inspirer and the Thought.

'Tis by degrees insensible and slow,
The chrysal worm assumes gay wings and flies;
'Tis by the same, must torpid Sinners grow
Adoring Saints, and holy Seraphs rise.

O cease not Thou due nutriment to lend,
To let the beam of heavenly wisdom shine!
The rest to HIM, on whom events depend,
Submit; assur'd, a glorious Crown is thine.

The ESTIMATE: or,

Reflexions on Temporal Good and Evil.
1763.

I. FAITH and Affection juftly God requires
Of man, fo form'd with reafon and defires.
The Slave in chains, the Monarch on the throne,
The Saint, whom glories amaranthin crown,
The bleffed Orders of eternal day,
Muft Him, who rules the univerfe, obey.
Profane Neglect, Concupifcence and Pride
Plague both offenders and the World befide;
With deep corruption taint created Good,
Alone dilutable with fweat and blood.
Neglect, Concupifence and Pride profane
Made this our fyftem, as we find it, vain.
Hence gayeft life is like a funny glade,
Where ev'ry floating vapor flings a fhade.
But as the vapors, by diftilling fhow'rs,
Refresh the verdures and enrich the flow'rs;
Pains, difappointments exercife the mind,
And render Virtue noble and refin'd;
Benignly temper Pleafure's fervid breath,
Which elfe, like mildew, fheds abortive death.

Providence

Providence kindly made our welkin scowl,
To wake and awe the dark erroneous soul;
Shook into mortal frailty Nature's frame,
Whence all our pains and all our sorrows came;
Like thorns and brambles, planted when Man
  fell,
To guard offenders from the road to Hell:
Kindly severe to save, (O noble view!)
Sinners and those, whom Sinners might undo.
For Sin, o'erflowing, deluge-like extends;
Nor know we where the spreading ruin ends.

Then wherefore mourn a Life not over gay;
Fly swift, not giddily, my hours away!
Come, useful Sorrows!—They, who suffer most,
May reap an harvest equal to their cost:
They, who the Curse, impos'd in mercy, prove,
May learn to dread God's anger from his love;
And, rais'd by trial arduous and complete,
Become at last, by kind correction great.

1. Consider those, whom God's blest spirit
  warm'd;
In whom divine benevolency charm'd;
Fit, as may seem, alone for holy Heaven;
Yet to the World for its Salvation given;
Apostles, Martyrs; they affliction found!
Their hallow'd blood imbru'd this cursed ground!
                                  See,

See, and with thine compare what ills they bore;
And learn to murmur and blaspheme no more.

Again, see those, to ev'ry mischief keen;
Who Virtue fiercely injure and malign;
Like subtil Vipers, lurking in the dust,
With deadly venom arm'd to grieve the Just;
See those, their grandeur vying with their guilt!
But ponder first; then envy, if Thou wilt.

All's by permission of supreme decree:
For due probation Sinners must be free.
In weight and number shall reward be given:
No fraud, no force eludes the Judge of Heaven.

Our blest Redeemer, our adored Guide,
Groan'd on a Cross, and like a felon dy'd.
If He so suffer'd, when he man became,
Let Folly blush to think affliction shame.
Affliction chosen thro' regard to *Fit*,
In firm obedience, is divinely great;
At once it strengthens and severely tries
Virtue expos'd, and stript of all disguise,
In Life's gymnastics to deserve renown,
And then receive an everlasting Crown.

Souls, never try'd, may glory as they can,
And rashly judge; but Trial shews the Man.

Say, what is Virtue, ever calm, unprov'd;
By pain or pleasure scarce a passion mov'd?
What thank have They, what merit, being good,
Who have no plea for erring if they wou'd?
They fair for Pride or Interest may appear,
Kind without cost, and without trust sincere.

Like wild Romancers, pigmy Souls at ease
Monsters create and conquer as they please.
Fantastic children, among Toy-things bred,
Angle for Whales, chain Lions with a thread:
Untutor'd Fancy all its wishes gains,
Nor ever dreams of dangers or of pains.
Thus flatter'd of themselves and others too,
No wonder Pigmies think them Giants true.
Mature Experience better knowledge brings,
Awakes from notions to contemplate Things;
True fear, true fortitude at once inspires;
And warns to rule aversions and desires.

Affliction teaches reason to command;
At once it tries and strengthens us to stand:
While in the Champion, whom oppressions bruise,
Victorious Virtue Heav'n delighted views.

2. " But grant, you cry, some from affliction
   " gain
" More good, than recompenses all their pain;

" Does not affliction often overflow,
" And overwhelm a noble Soul in woe ?"

It does, I grant,—And, while God leaves them
    free,
Mankind will deviate ; crimes will ever be.
Yet is its End, as fact declares, to prove
Virtue decay'd, and bid repentance move :
Its toils and dangers give us strength and skill
To hate and shun offences, if we will.
Whoe'er succumb in agony and fear,
In pleasure likely wou'd be insincere ;
Perhaps wou'd sin thro' wanton folly more
Than e'er affliction made them sin before.
For riches, honors, pleasures let them pray ;
God knows their Int'rest better far than they :
To grant their wishes were to grant a curse
So great, that Hell could not inflict a worse.

Pleasure or Pain must try our Virtue still :
Oft souls affected both united feel.
Pleasure's more dangerous, destitute of guard ;
And its sweet Trial is its own reward.
Pain's more secure ; but if intense, 'tis dire ;
'Tis like the Chymist's purifying fire :
For truth 'tis borne, or can't be shun'd at all ;
While Pleasure's woo'd, tho' to its Votary's fall.

So

So Pain, if virtuous, is chief merit still;
And Pleasure vicious is the deepest ill.
One must us try; Then which in Reason's view
Is best?—Why! Pain is safest, noblest too.

Pain may toss Virtue, rough, on floods of woe;
Yet still is Pleasure Virtue's direst foe.
By furious storms the Vessel oft is drove
From *Scylla's* rocks and *Circe's* odious love.
Pain may wreck Virtue, true! But Virtue brave
Rises exalted from the whelming wave:
Insidious Pleasure might far worse beguile;
True *Circe* she, with fatal voice and smile!

3. " I still aver, that Fortune might adorn
" The charms of Virtue; and exalt her horn."

Like other Beauties, doubtless, Virtue charms
Most irresistibly, when splendor arms.
But too, too many Fortune's Gifts entice
To leave the Lady for the Harlot, Vice.
What State to pray for underneath the sun
I cannot tell!——O God! thy will be done!

II. Alas! how futile all, our Fancies frame
Of *Beauty, Opulency, Honor, Fame!*
Obtaining all, and more than thought conceives,
Than *Mah'met* feign'd or Mussulman believes,

There

There still wants something—O that something!
    more
Than Vice attains in all Creation's store!
Nay, Virtue too, is here too far distress'd
To harbor *Happiness*, celestial Guest!
When pure Perfection, foil'd by Sin, withdrew,
The radiant Goddess from this region flew.
She dwells on high: her beams Life's frailties
    shroud;
She only shines, by glances, thro' a cloud;
From her celestial sphere she scorns to bend;
No earthly charm can tempt her to descend:
Deigns not her presence on a golden throne,
In regal purple, or in sacred lawn;
Not in a princely coronet enshrin'd;
Nor with a martial shoulder-knot entwin'd;
Fills no gold box, nor blazes in a star;
Rides not huzza'd in corporation chair;
Exhales not from stain'd paste-board at Quadrille;
Soft Beauty's kisses, or the Poet's quill.
Not Beauty, Opulency, Empire, Fame,
Include the essence of the sacred dame.
Superb Delusions! poor vain-glorious boast!
By seeking them, what Crowds themselves have
    lost!

1. Survey with candor joys, which them supply,
Who glow with Beauty, or for Beauty sigh.

                           Advancing

Advancing, lo, the Charmer, smiling, young;
Gay *Strephon* list'ning to her silver tongue:
How fine her features! and how freshly blows
The sweetest hue of lily blent with rose!
Her eyes like morn; her cherry lips, like spring,
Breath love and odor on the breeze's wing.
See him in extasy peruse her charms!
Fix'd, panting, trembling, fainting for her arms.
See her now blushing, yielding, while he pleads;
Both fill'd with bliss, which utterance exceeds.
But, O! the Change!—When passions fiercely
    burn,
Soon cold satiety succeeds in turn.
Cast o'er the Soul that dull benumbing chain,
How palls the joy! how grows the union pain!
To all her charms, and ev'n endearments, dead,
He soon neglects her stale familiar bed;
She (worse than death!) beholds a Rival rais'd,
And love-enthron'd, where late her glory blaz'd;
Her only portion to despair; or worse,
To retrospect her folly with remorse.
Perhaps the youthful She, as foul in mind
As fair in form, proves silly, grows unkind;
Is loud, is stubborn; neither knows nor cares
For nuptial duties; but by choice still errs:
Her coarse behaviour renders Both the tale,
The spiteful sport of neighboring Town and Vale.
                           How

How must the Husband, curst with such a mate!
Drag life in bitterness, and mourn his fate!
Ah, worse! if yet, more dear than self, his Race
Involv'd are too in ruin and disgrace!
Wretched indeed! The depth of his distress
No heart can think, but his; no tongue express.

Besides, an endless changing madness rules
The beauteous and the beauty-loving Fools:
The vicious pleasure, soon as gain'd, expires:
Their Life's a chace twixt shadows and desires.
Virtue and Sense, which make Love's passion pure,
Alone exalt the flame and feed it to endure.

Yet deem not Beauty, altho' frail, invain;
Important blessings, many, fill her train.
Lively delight springs at the charming view;
And sweetly pleas'd is she in pleasing you.
Nothing so charming in the world we find,
Except the Goddess in her beams enshrin'd,
The heav'nly Soul, endu'd with angel-grace,
Divinely beaming thro' the curious case:
And far indeed o'er Beauty we extol
The fair, divinely-amiable Soul.

2. Should you in Opulence with *Cræsus* vie;
And each destroying angel still pass by;

Your

Your dwelling pompous as the coftly dome,
Where *Mary*'s Idol bends the knees of Rome :
Let views around excel Elyfian fcenes ;
Hills fweetly fmile with fineft blooms and greens ;
Vales fhoot bleft groves, with chryftal ftreams
       among ;
Birds, richly plum'd, extol melodious fong :
Your fumptuous table load, each day you dine,
With dainty viands and delicious wine :
Let all your moments gently fteal away
In quaint amufement, company and play :
And, when you chufe at intervals to ride
For rural paftime, and to blaze your pride,
Let stateliest fteeds your gorgeous chariot pull ;
And in retinue rival the *Mogul* :
Alas, if Virtue does not gild thy horn,
And manly Wifdom guide thee and adorn,
In vain does Fortune lend her golden fhield,
Poor is the pleafure all thefe luxuries yield.

  Yet what can Opulence, but pleafure give ;
And eafe diftreffes, partly, while we live ?
Abftract thefe ufes, millions, golden ftore,
Are arrant trafh, as pebbles on the fhore.
And, ah, if tempt they to relinquifh God,
Abufe his Creatures and deferve his rod,
To fcorn his gracious overtures, and then
Incur his Vengeance—Horror ! ftop my pen!

                           Not

Not only poor the pleasure, riches gain;
The Owner's folly makes the blessing bane,
When no fair child of wealth the Fool can bless,
But the base-born inchantress, lewd Excess.
Exotic-like the puny tendril grows;
The chymic essence ill betrays the nose;
At First, a fragrant redolence instils;
But, long continu'd, pangs corrodes and kills.

Pleasure, indeed, I wou'd not discommend,
Were she not often a perfidious friend:
Nor spurn at riches, heap'd in due degree,
Pernicious neither to the state nor me.
I grant fair Pleasure's blandishments should draw,
But ever modifi'd by wisdom's law.
Propense to err, temerity is such;
Some love the Dame too little, some to much.
You need no instance: If you do, behold
The Miser's tatters and the Fribble's gold.
Or note a contrast more affecting yet,
The frozen Nun, and all-inflam'd Coquette.
Lo, Both, whate'er they speciously pretend,
Are vain Contemners of great Nature's end:
'Tis plain, that Nature meant the course between
To mind ends noble, nor forget the mean.
All passions tend, if rightly understood,
To Individual, universal Good.

Int'rest

Int'reſt combines the univerſal Frame;
For individuals mutual ſuccor claim.
The truly wiſe endeavor mutual eaſe;
Are always pleas'd, and always aim to pleaſe:
Their paſſions all, in Charity, obey
The Holy Monarch's beatific ſway.

Virtue, which under pain is leaſt diſtreſt,
Can alſo reliſh real pleaſure beſt.
Without it, pleaſure is not only vain;
But fatal too, more dangerous than pain:
With it, does pleaſure happily improve;
And grow divine, and ſoar to holy Love,
The perfect pleaſure, *That*, where all ſhou'd aim,
The heav'nly Happineſs, the Bliſs ſupreme.
With Virtue, Riches purchaſe pure delight;
Repel diſtreſs and inſolence and ſpight;
Extended piouſly to Miſ'ry's aid,
Purchaſe pure joy and glory, ne'er to fade.
Such noble benefits by Virtue flow
From things, which, Vice-abus'd, pour endleſs
    woe.

3. Suppoſe you Empire happineſs complete?
Your wiſh be crown'd: Go mount the regal ſeat!
The proud Aſſyrian ſhall revive in Thee:
Adoring Nations hail and bend the knee.

Remotest shores and undiscover'd waves
Shall usher myriads, falling prone thy slaves.
Thy pompous palace ev'ry Clime shall fill
With Nature's pride, with Art's sublimest skill:
Fish yield their pearls, their spice the balmy Trees;
Thy Spinners, Worms; thy Potters, the Chinese:
Painting the magic of her hand display;
And plastic Sculpture, all but life convey:
The polish'd needle and the florid loom,
Conspire to deck and glorify thy room:
Not all the grandeurs of Imperial state
Can charm a pain, or stay one stroke of fate:
Immense dependencies and arduous care
Permit not happiness to enter there:
Firm Virtue hardly bears from sinking down
Beneath the dizzy circle of a Crown.

    Kings, who for Evil rule, contemning laws,
Make war on subjects, direr than on foes:
Not worse the crime of subjects, who rebel,
When patriot Kings, revering laws, rule well.
As Small for Great, so Great exist for Small:
If must some perish, better one than all.
Justice shou'd govern! Tyrants, past debate,
Are the worst Rebels, Traitors to the State:
A Right divine his pow'r to misapply
  The Greatest Cæsar had no more than I.
                            Jehovah

JEHOVAH reigns! Inferior Lords fhou'd know
Him only abfolute, Him Source of law.
Forever juft is all, that He ordains;
Good univerfal his defign, He reigns.

If little Villains fwing by one confent,
While great ones glory in a monument;
'Tis Fortune's triumph. Peep behind the fcene:
Wou'd you be *Dives*, Sir, or *Lazarus* then?
Stripp'd off the armor, Goddefs Fortune gave,
Th' *Achilles* toffes on a fiery wave;
A blafted wreck on the infernal Sea,
As furious and implacable as He.

The Villain, who dominion does attain,
Is a deftructive curs'd Leviathan;
Lewdly enjoying his enormous ftate,
His mercy's cruel, and, his love like hate:
Profufe beneficence and lofty praife
From him are fatal, as a lure betrays.
Againft conviction, arm'd with pow'r and wealth,
He madly riots, while indulg'd with health;
Derides the Ruler of the ftarry fphere,
With all the righteous hope, the wicked fear;
'Till, feiz'd by death, his foul to hell is hurl'd,
His memory curfed by an injur'd world.

Glorious

Glorious indeed is pow'r, employ'd to bless;
To punish Vice and to relieve distress:
Hence virtuous Rulers shall for ever shine
Beatify'd in glory, crown'd divine.

4. How oft do they, whose souls to Fame aspire,
Incur destruction in their fond desire?
Few, while they live, obtain the boon, they crave;
And blows Fame loud, who hears her in the grave?
Oft, cou'd her trumpet shake the unbrac'd drum,
Curses and scoffs wou'd dread as thunder come;
Nor cou'd her sweetest harmony asswage
One penal pang, or sooth a Dæmon's rage.

In common sense, what can the Hero claim?
Fool, Madman, Murderer, killing, kill'd, for Fame!
Supremely mad! his soul, in ev'ry spring,
Aspires to mischief, worthy of a King:
The very scenes of his amusement shew
His love of horror and delight in woe:
Like English *Edward*, or olympian *Jove*,
In flame and thunder he addresses love;
Before God's altar, clad in armor, stands;
To the Creator spreads destroying hands:
His Person, palace and magnific car
Wear all alike the boisterous air of war.

Ah,

Ah, how his sentiments will change with place!
What's glory now will then emerge disgrace.
When He no more shall cruelly annoy,
When the destroyer fiends and worms destroy,
His glory shall be shame: He then shall find
Each gall-fill'd measure meted back in kind.
The sumptuous Castle, which his folly built
To bear his name (grand monument of guilt!)
Shall stand deserted, 'till the trophy'd wall,
Besieg'd with Vengeance, into ruin fall;
Grown o'er with ivy, roost obscenest fowls;
A lodge of serpents, and a court of owls.
One Clown amusing others, as from work
He strides along and swings his shoulder'd fork,
Cries—" Here liv'd *Bravo*; such his martial life;
" Such his domain; and such a one his Wife,"
As cordial joy the story now affords
From lips of Clowns as from the lips of Lords.
So Glory sets!—The Grave (by lawful claim)
The Carcase swallows; and Oblivion, Fame.

But they, who, truly brave, War's front defy
Greatly resolv'd to conquer or to die,
Who not for Fame alone, but in disdain
Of haughty wrongs, tyrannic pride to rein,
Obey the trump, when Justice bids obey;
And but for mercy sternly draw and slay;

       Divinely

Divinely rous'd in Virtue's cause to deal
The keen impressions of decisive steel:
Such may indulge their passion for Renown:
Their generous pride celestial wreaths shall crown.

All passions, which with God's imperial Will
Concur devoutly, must be laudable.
As all are impious, and to mis'ry tend,
Without design'd subservience to that end.

The tuneful Poet, who sublimely sings
Of Beauties, Heroes, Patriots, Nobles, Kings,
(If Adulation, with perswasive tongue,
Demurely servile, patronizes wrong;
Or Satire, fell, shall on the worthy pour
Opprobrious pasquils with demoniac roar)
May reap a harvest to his culture due
Offence from Many, but applause from Few.
Nor must the Genius, like a comet-flame,
Eccentric soaring, adoration claim:
That, like the Sun, which from a constant sphere
Effulgent beams, enliv'ning all the year,
Deserves applause; and there will mortals vow
Their best devotion to the laurell'd brow.
Fame's gaudiest plumes perhaps too often wing
Those poison'd arrows on Jehovah's string,
Immoral Poets; while the crowd despise
His choicest blessings in the good and wise.

Vain

Vain senseless world! how little dost thou know
Thy real good! O worthy of thy woe!
But short's the date of that perverse applause,
Which from a local, temporal, folly flows:
Succeeding times, unprejudic'd, detest
The poison strong, and scorn the feeble jest;
And blame their Fathers, tho' themselves pursue,
With equal folly, bards as bad, but new.

Ye high-soul'd bards! weigh vulgar praise and
   blame;
Weigh and contemn the stupid buzz of Fame;
Contemn her poor erroneous hate and love:
Revere the righteous Arbiter above:
Next him, the Few of sense and candor prize;
And only dread the censure of the wise:
Hence shall ye win the noblest crown of Fame,
A genuine glory, sanctify'd from shame;
Truly immortal; which, when Earth decays,
In Heav'n shall rise, and shine with ten-fold blaze.

5. Behold in Nature's present usual course,
Vice leads to meaness, mis'ry and remorse.
Those vicious passions, violent as blind,
Which touch the rights and beings of mankind;
Which rove for pleasure, struggle to look down
On bending mobs, or call more dirt their own;
        Such

Such must the essence of true bliss destroy;
Disquiet self, society annoy.
Passions ridiculous also make unblest;
Altho' their chief concernment is a jest.
The vain Coquette, when beauty fades, cou'd die;
The Dotard trembles, if a Raven cry:
The Courtier and the Lover dread a frown:
The Poet dreads the Censure of the Town:
A thronged *Smithfield* or unwelcome Air
Afflicts the Farmer with profound despair;
Not that he wants, but wishes—(no great harm)
To be, at length, the Landlord of a Farm:
Just as the Landlord, anxious to be great,
With restless ardor meditates a Seat.

But comfort here! If such vain whimsies teaze;
New toy or ditty will the Baby please.
Call *Pyrrha* charming: For *Canidia's* ail
Apply some slander or prodigious tale:
The careless smile, a Wanton flings away,
Will serve to make her dying Lover gay:
That pow'rful nod, which golden days portends,
Inchants the Courtier to forget his friends:
The Farmer bowzes, if the Market's dear;
The chosen Patriot is, in hope, a Peer.

6. To

6. To view man's little, mean, preposterous aims
And vain importance, modesty ashames.
To view this grand, immense, stupendous Frame,
And muse the pow'r and goodness whence it came,
Sinks man to nothing!—When thy works I see,
O God! I wonder thou regardest me!
For men to boast of Wisdom and of Worth,
Yet not adore the Lord of Heav'n and Earth,
How mad! how vain!—Do not all blessings fall
From that right hand, which opening filleth all?
Who can be so ungenerous to offend
So good a Lord, so bountiful a Friend?
Who dares against that Majesty rebel,
Which frowning kills, which breathing kindles Hell?

7. If vile illusions captivate the heart;
Alas! they well compensate the desert;
For baubles if we study, toil and bleed,
They all forsake us in our greatest need;
Leave us to learn too late, and long lament,
Folly is justly its own punishment.
Those gewgaw trifles, priz'd in health and ease,
In pain and sorrow lose the charm to please.
Earth's noblest Comforts, at the dying hour,
Seem names, not natures, Phantoms without pow'r.

And

And oft, what vainly we as Virtue boaſt,
Emerges then but venial ſin at moſt.
The leaſt good action, worthy of a Saint,
A cup of of water to relieve the faint,
Scoop'd from the ſurface of a bubbling ſpring,
Excels the glories of the *Pruſſian* King.

Say, what the meed, the deepeſt villain gains
By all his guilty artifice and pains?
In vain the wretch for happineſs contends:
No happineſs finds He, who God offends.
No!—When Illuſion, vaniſhing, is fled,
Joy ſhuns his dwelling, and repoſe his bed:
He wiſhes oft, and ſeeks, thro' his own blood,
Annihilation, as the only good.

8. O what is Happineſs? Thou Muſe divine!
Declare; for Thou canſt tell: The light is thine!

9. No Circumſtances Happineſs create,
Without a Temper ſuited to the ſtate:
No Temper, without Circumſtances fit,
And ſocial Aid, finds happineſs complete:
Heav'n wiſely plac'd what *Happineſs* we call,
In *Plenty, Health* and *Rectitude*: in *All.*
Plenty and *Health* on *Rectitude* depend;
Becauſe *Probation* is the *ſovereign End.*

O   10. Ah,

10. Ah, then! what hope in this depraved
 state,
Where vicious Love engenders vicious Hate;
And vicious Hate and Love break Nature's Law,
Which juftly dooms Depravity to woe?
What can we hope?—Why, juft the fate we find!
Convinc'd of this, my Soul! be all refign'd!

11. *Virtue*, fair image of th' Almighty Sire,
Confent divine of reafon and defire,
Virtue refin'd, ev'n chriftian light and love,
Sent with the Holy Spirit from above,
Virtue alone can happinefs receive;
Virtue alone true happinefs can give.
No demonftration plainer! All *Delight*
Confifts in *Love*; And *Virtue*, loving Right,
(Supremely *God*, then *All*, above, below,
In *due degree*, *due Love of All we know*)
Virtue alone can with *delight* impel
To follow *Duty*, and be *pleafed well*:
Virtue alone, purfuing *Duty's* road,
Can claim *benevolence* from Man or God:
Virtue alone can fweet *Communion fhare*
With God and Saints; and *perfect glory bear.*
This all is plain: And juft is it as clear,
That *Vice* admits *no happinefs fincere.*

Vice

Vice must be wretched: for the least degree
Of mere *Reluctance* smacks of misery:
And bold *Rebellion*, seizing guilty joys,
The more it prospers, more itself destroys.
Admit it triumphs on this cursed ball,
Remuneration soon will settle all.
If *Virtue* groans, with pious patience wait
That grand decision of a *future state:*
God will in *that*, whate'er men do in *this*,
Doom *Vice* to *woe*, and *Virtue* crown with *bliss:*
In endless *woe* shall wicked Souls be bound;
All plagu'd, all plaguing, sunk in *Hell* profound:
Eternal *bliss* the Righteous shall enjoy,
Uprais'd to *Heav'n*, the new-born earth and sky:
All bless'd, all blessing, as God's laws ordain,
Bliss shall fill all, and God delighted reign.

12. O God! I ask not Pleasures, Honors,
    Wealth!
Grant Competence, Tranquillity and Health!
But whether storm or sunshine intervene,
Almighty Father, Virtue grant within!
O grant me Virtue! my supreme request!
I know, that Virtue must at last be blest:
I know that Thou, most righteous Lord! at last,
Wilt fully recompense all trials past;
                          Wilt

Wilt love thy lovers, with indulgence own,
With favor comfort, and with glory crown:
O grant me Virtue to extent divine!
Until my soul thy perfect Image shine!
Then kindle, Vengeance; and, from pole to pole,
Devoted Worlds to second Chaos roll;
I, fix'd on Thee, the everlasting Rock,
Will stand, unmov'd, the universal shock!

AN ODE.

BE still, sporting flocks; lowly silent obey!
   O listen, ye careless! come home, ye that stray!
Your shepherd he calls, who your hunger supplies
By day and by night, ever watchful his eyes.
O'er the vales and the mountains he gently does lead
To pastures of health, where you joyfully feed:
There suffers his lambs unmolested to rove
By rivers of pleasure, and fountains of love.
The simple he warneth, when danger appears;
The weak in his bosom he tenderly rears;

And

And supports, as he slowly conducts her along,
The heavy-pac'd female, that's laden with young.
The blood-thirsty wolf is both cunning and bold;
But his angry voice frights the wolf from the fold.
The bear and the lion, he crushes their jaws,
And rescues the prey from their merciless paws.
Nor this for your welfare your shepherd disdains:
Be grateful, ye flocks! and compensate his pains.
From his fold or his pastures ne'er carelesly stray;
But love your good shepherd, his calling obey.
The wanton, the wand'ring, forgetful poor sheep,
The wolf may destroy, or a fall from a steep.
'Tis safest and happiest to feed and to lie
Not far from his side, nor from under his eye.

AN ODE.

SEE! see! the lovely rosy Morn
   Diffuse prolific beams
O'er flow'ry meadows, springing corn,
   And painted silver streams;

While rove the flocks o'er hill and dale,
   With herb luxuriant spread;
And blooming forests to the gale
   Delicious odors shed,

                              Methinks

Methinks again fair *Eden* grows,
Her scenes and pleasures dawn,
As at Creation's birth she rose,
When first the day-spring shone.

See! Love and Pleasure now preside,
Great Nature's chief delight!
All seem to boast immortal pride,
And hope eternal light.

O Pow'r immense! that still supplies,
At wisdom's vast expence,
Glories, exciting, grand surprize:
But why recal them hence?

Has Innocence such charms with thee?
For her is all this cost?
When man profan'd thy sacred tree,
She fled,—The world was lost.

Yes!—Innocence my God admires;
Where'er she deigns to dwell,
His presence happiness inspires;
If absent she—'tis hell.

Ye lovely visions! (for no more
Substantial good I call)

Sweet

Bleft Innocence difdains our fhore,
Then perifh muft ye all.

'Tis but a gleam of Grace beftows
This bloom on life decay'd:
All tranfient like the Summer rofe,
All flourifh, and all fade.

Soon Death fhall force the painful figh,
And load the mournful bier;
To beauty fhut the charmed eye,
To melody the ear.

Low wrapt in hallow'd mould fhall fleep
The fwain, forgot his lay.
No bofom heave, no eye-lid weep!
Prepare and come away!

ODE. *To Mufic.*

MUsic, tune thy filver ftrings!
    Notes melodious, gently roll!
Softly, foftly, wake the Soul,
Awake her fympathetic fprings!

Slow and tender, sweet and shrill,
With pleas'd and mild attention fill:
Strong and bolder when they grow,
We feel the bosom beat and glow;
Joy, joy through all the nerves rebounds,
Which dance and thrill to charming sounds.

Pleasure like the virgin's breast,
Fond and chaste, and soft and gay,
Inspires the passions of the blest,
And chases ruder thoughts away.
Virtue lifts her brow serene:
Chearful Peace and raptur'd Love
Adorn the bright inchanting scene,
As on a festive day above.

Away! far hence away! Prophane!
Defile not Music's purer breath:
Your skill may gratify the vain,
And chear the odious ways of death.
Think not joy to you confin'd;
Brutes possess a brutal mind:
To sordid natures filth is sweet;
So folly goes with fools for wit:
Ravens admire the croaking voice;
The meaner taste, the meaner choice.

But

But happier natures, mov'd by finer springs,
  (Like weaned lambs, that nicely feed
  On choicest herbs, in freshest mead;
  Or bees, that sip the blooming thyme)
  Enjoy a relish more sublime,
Which purest pleasure brings.

Away, Austere! whose peevish pride,
Another's pleasure can't abide;
With spite and censure like to burst,
With base ill-nature greatly curst;
Least virtuous, when ye most pretend
To act and speak as Virtue's friend.

Be mine the pleasing social road
Thro' nature's flowrieft paths to God.
With modest awe I'll cull each sweet,
And spread my thanks before his feet.

ODE. *To Music.*

WHEN first the mild Orient, from mountain
    top seen,
Strews heaven with roses, bespangles the green,
                              The

The Shepherd his rural employment renews;
From his cott, see! his footsteps have brush'd off
    the dews.
His call wakes the village, his fold open stands;
His snowy-fleec'd innocents whiten the lands.
In air, the wing'd songsters mix'd voices employ;
The groves how melodious! the fields laugh with
    joy!
The glossy-bloom'd flow'rets depastur'd with bees,
All hums around Carmel, and trills the soft
    breeze.
His mellow pipe tunes, and the hollow vale fills
With music, which echo prolongs in the hills.
He sooths his own bosom, and vents to the air
The passion he shames to reveal to the Fair:
And thus, if his Shepherdess scornful appears,
He steals to her heart, while he pleases her ears:
The maids of the village attentive stand still,
Forgotten the milk-pail, the distaff, and wheel;
All panting and sighing, the Shepherd's notes roll
So tunefully tenderly strong on the soul.

 In Pleasure's pomps, and gay resorts,
  'Tis Music's pow'rful song
 Dispels the artificial cares of Courts,
  And all the pale-ey'd throng.

Joy, enraptur'd joy she brings,
    And blameless joy inspires;
Love quivers round on purple wings,
    And all the social grand Desires.
Without her brisk inspiring airs,
    The splendid scenes would fade;
Ev'n Pleasure languish with fantastic cares,
    And sighing droop her ornamented head.

    When to the sacred Dome we go,
And tread with decent rev'rence hallow'd ground,
Like some good angel's voice the solemn organs
    blow,
And waft our souls to heav'n amid the sound.
    Holy gratitude and love
    Holy as the flames above,
    From pure seraphic fires,
    Rise, from ev'ry bosom rise,
    A grateful incense to the skies,
    While Music's breath inspires.

Mysterious pow'r of tuneful sound!
Thyself a proof of what thou tell'st abroad!
What ear so dull hath heard thee, and not found
In thee the good, the wise, the pow'rful God?

                    AN

An Hymn.

Never-failing, overflowing,
    Fountain of celestial joy!
Numberless thy gifts bestowing,
Ev'ry moment we enjoy.

How forgetful, how ungrateful,
Vain and scornful are we?
How provoking, and how hateful,
Are the thoughts of man to thee!

Wrapt in business, or in pleasure,
For this world, this age, we live:
Better thoughts require more leisure
Than our appetites will give.

Whence, ah whence! this inconsistence?
Man's first wish is to obtain
Endless, happy, bright existence:
Why neglect the means to gain?

Proves not this an erring creature?
Reason, call th' eternal pow'r
To enlighten, strengthen nature,
And thy proper end secure.

Childish ever thou, unaided;
Ever confident, yet wrong;
Humoursome, and scarce persuaded
By thy Maker's warning tongue.

Holy Spirit! be thy dwelling,
In my bosom's humble shrine!
Luminary, far excelling
All the orbs that brightly shine!

Tho' with curious inclination,
Human science I explore;
Shew me, chief, thy great salvation;
Teach me purely to adore.

Other knowledge all must vanish;
All its uses center here:
Pious knowledge will replenish,
And adorn our heav'nly sphere.

Blind, how blind with all our science!
Profit pays not half the toil:
Nature yields no brib'd compliance;
Deep she hides the precious spoil.

Truths unuseful or undoing,
Sacred Providence does hide;

Kindly

Kindly stays us from our ruin,
Mortifies our foolish pride.

Tho' with curious inclination,
Human science I explore;
Shew me, shew me, thy salvation!
Teach me purely to adore.

David's *Song of* Triumph.

Arise!
Arise, JEHOVAH! with thy awful nod
Scatter thy trembling enemies abroad!
Like chaff in whirlwinds borne away,
The Wicked in thy wrath decay.

Him, lo! the glorious Cherubs bore:
On wings of rapid winds He came:
Fury and Terror flew before;
Earth shook, and Heav'n's eternal frame!

Horrid darkness roll'd around;
Tumultuous back the roaring Ocean fled,
And naked left his oozy bed;
Blue lightnings flam'd along the ground.

Our enemies in difarray,
Pale and crying, fled away.

JEHOVAH is my ftrength and pow'r,
My lamp of unextinguifhable light,
My fhield, my rock, my lofty tow'r;
He guards my life, and guides my ways aright:

    Train'd by his almighty care,
    Invincible I rufh to war;
    Swifter than the mountain roe,
    Stronger than the ftrongeft bow.

I have purfu'd—I have deftroy'd—
    I turned not again,
Until my flaughter'd enemies lay void
Of genial life, in heaps upon the plain.

My vanquifh'd foes no more fhall rife:
Their necks beneath my foot-fteps lie.
Omnipotence, which rules the fkies,
Shall fet his fervant's glory high.

Then thanks, JEHOVAH! thanks to Thee,
Whofe tender mercy fets me free!
To Earth's remoteft ends I'll fing
Thy praifes, great eternal King!

                              AN

AN HYMN,

O Rise, my soul! and rise, my song!
Inspiring rapture bear along!
On wings of heav'nly joy I soar,
The Throne Almighty to adore!

O place me far above the wrongs
Of cruel hearts, and busy tongues;
Above the reach of hate and guile,
The tyrant's frown, the traitor's smile!

Then will thy servant, Lord, proclaim
Thy awful laws to the remotest shore;
And people, strangers to thy holy name,
Thee, Thee, O God eternal, shall adore!

Praise, O my soul! extol his praise!
His faithful promise cannot fail.
Illumin'd with his glorious rays,
And strengthen'd, I shall still prevail.

O! for his honor zealous be;
He never can be false to thee.
So when these ruins of this world
Shall be again to Chaos hurl'd,
And vengeance flame with wrath divine,
Peace, joy, and glory, shall be thine.

On the *Divine Wisdom* in distributing *Pleasure* and *Pain*.

A Fragment.

BEhold how wisely *pains* and *pleasures* blend,
To keep us steady to the sovereign End!

See fools of rapture, flaming to pursue
Joys, fancy paints in fascinating view,
Scarce sooner siezing the delusive charm,
Than all their ardor latent banes disarm.

Nay, ev'n the wise, who but indulge as fit
In sober joys, which are most exquisite,
At frequent intervals find some allay
Suggest, they are but Beings of a day.

As in that season, when the greens and blooms
Clothe Nature gay, and freshly breathe perfumes,
Each bird of music amorous carol sings;
And Insect-lovers frisk on filmy wings;
So gentle youth as carelesly employ
Unnumber'd days in sprightly acts of joy:
Yet oft the floating cloud and chilling blast
Foretel th' arrival of old age at last.

On that delight, which finer spirits know
In social union, friendship's tender glow,

P ('That

(That dear delight, if ought on earth be dear,
To make a parting worthy of a tear,
To heave the bosom with a longing sigh,
Or cause one wish to linger when we die)
On that delight, alas, what ills attend!
Those sharpest ills, derived from a friend!
At best the blessing hangs on chance and breath;
While oft th' attending woes are worse than death.

Perhaps too few have any soul at all
For what, with emphasis, we *friendship* call:
Dull, or diverted by some vulgar flame,
Few rise to friendship's elevated aim.
Interest's caresses, Vanity's pretence
And Envy's wiles admit no friendly sense.
Ev'n ardent souls, which friendly seem to burn,
Oft waste, and grow more ashes in the urn;
Or, like a wandering meteorous fire,
By sudden glances kindle and expire.

Geat *Alexander*, greatly mad and vain,
Stab'd his dear friend, then wept his *Clytus* slain;
So numbers do!—Alas, it boots to know
How more a friend is cruel than a Foe.
Beware of friendships!—the capricious shun!
What ends in pain were better ne'er begun.

Friendship's

Friendship's the most sublime of blessings given
To man, the nearest in approach to Heaven;
But noblest things, perverted, grow the worst.
To find our Heav'n a Hell is most accurst.

O happy they, who, worthy friendship's name,
United long, are constantly the same!
Like rows of columns, some fair structure's base,
Each lends to each at once support and grace:
Or liker stars, whose mutual pulses keep
Their gyres undevious thro' th' etherial deep,
They move harmonious shedding genial fire,
'Till, as shall stars, they gloriously expire.
Such happy souls, ev'n when their joys are spent,
Repose in union, full of sweet content:
Their tranquil tempers feel no ruder woe,
Than those, which age and frailty must bestow;
And pure contentment oft prolongs their stay
In life, 'till late, when calm they glide away.
Happy are they, if Happiness e'er deigns
To cast one beam on earth's devoted plains.

But ah, these highest joys can only move
To wish for joys eternal, far above!
They soon pass by; they just salute the heart,
Awake the warm desire, and then depart.

No

No skill no might exempts the wise and brave
From frailty's law, from mis'ry and the grave.
Great *Mithridates*, wise as well as great,
And brave as wise, experienc'd dire defeat:
Ev'n poison's pow'r his science cou'd repel;
But by an executioner he fell.
Whilst rude *Goliath* boasts gigantic strength,
A pebble lays him shivering at his length.

Such are the frailties, rose in evil hour,
To shew Sin's nature, God's avenging pow'r:
Severe but kind monitions, vice to quell;
And virtue try and strengthen, to excel;
In due subservience to the glorious plan
Of trying, and at last redeeming man.

FINIS.